Broken, Yet Unstoppable

THE JOURNEY, STRUGGLES AND VICTORIES OF RUTH, NAOMI AND OUR KINSMAN- REDEEMER

JOAN E. MURRAY

Book cover designed by, Woodson Creative Studio.

Joan Murray Ministries & Seeds Of Hope Worldwide Missions

26340 FM 1736

Waller, TX 77848

281-398-2501

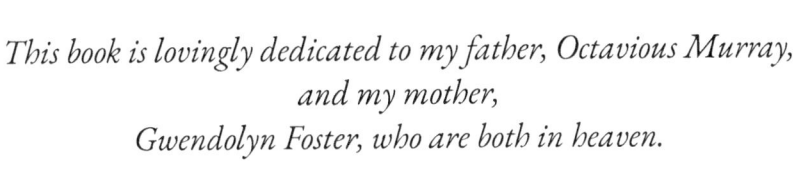

*This book is lovingly dedicated to my father, Octavious Murray,
and my mother,
Gwendolyn Foster, who are both in heaven.*

Acknowledgments

I am truly thankful to the Lord Jesus Christ for His deep inspiration, steady leadership, and priceless guidance in writing this book. With His help, I could examine my heart and assess what work needed to be done in my own personal life for the message of this book to touch the hearts of those who need to reconnect to Him. I am eternally grateful for His love and compassion toward me.

I thank my Board of Directors and the Joan Murray Ministries Team for their continued support, encouragement, and prayer each time I undertake another assignment to write the words that the Lord gives me.

I sincerely thank Rev. (Dr.) Isaac Egbewole, Polly Barker, Coleen Hanks, Danny and Griselda Martinez, and Leti Nava, for their time and commitment to read and endorse this book.

Praise for Broken, Yet Unstoppable

Joan has a God-given gift for bringing scripture to life, allowing one to apply it to diverse modern-day situations. If you, like me, have asked some "*Whys*" during the course of your life, this book is for you. If you live in brokenness and desire a new beginning, this book will help you trust God for restoration.

Chapter 8 states: "Jesus left the majesty of Heaven and its glorious splendor to enter broken humanity because love beckoned Him." He became broken yet unstoppable, so we, in our brokenness, can also be UNSTOPPABLE.

Learn how God will "put a plan in place that will take you into the future, not broken, bitter, poor, or oppressed but filled with joy and peace," as He did for Naomi. Meet our true Kinsman-Redeemer, Jesus, by acquiring this life-changing book.

BROKEN, YET UNSTOPPABLE is definitely a MUST-READ!

Leticia Perez-Nava,
Former Vice President/Regional Manager, International Financial Services, JPMorganChase
McAllen, Texas

As you read Joan E. Murray's book, *"Broken, Yet Unstoppable,"* you will be embraced by the arms of your Heavenly Father as He reveals His unwavering love for His children in life's journey. The story of Ruth and Naomi is thoroughly examined, and valuable insights into the complexities of resilience in adversity, moral integrity, and the enduring power of love, loyalty, and hope are exemplified.

This book is filled with testimonies of God's faithfulness and how heartbreak in the hands of our redeemer becomes a stepping stone to a miracle. The Holy Spirit will minister to your soul, and healing will occur. Even through your pain, loss, and unfaithfulness, God remains faithful and the source of love, healing, and redemption. He welcomes you home and reminds all weary and heavy-laden people that He will give them rest.

Pastors Daniel & Griselda Martinez
Templo Monte De Sion Internacional
San Juan, Texas

Thank you, Joan E. Murray, for doing the heavy lifting and studying to explain the history, background, and culture of the beloved story of Ruth. Joan takes us straight into the Word and helps us see that God's plan for redemption brings hope from despair and beauty from ashes. She reminds us that God is bigger than any crisis and that there is no path to victory apart from knowing Jesus. I highly recommend this book!

Polly Barker, Co-Founder
Katy Community Fellowship
Katy, Texas

Using the relationship journey of Ruth & Naomi, others from the Bible, and some personal stories from her own life, Joan connects and identifies with us in our most difficult seasons. She reminds us how God is indeed with us in our most painful journeys and even uses them mightily to deepen our relationship with Him.

She helps us better navigate some of life's most puzzling questions. More importantly, she helps us see the beautiful work the Lord can do in and through these hard things. In *"Broken, Yet Unstoppable,"* she uses biblical examples to reveal the hope found in Christ and to encourage and strengthen us in the "Whys."

Coleen Hanks, Co-Owner
Wet Pools, Inc.
Katy, Texas

Foreword

Absolutely, there is nothing that teaches better than the first-hand experience in our journey in life. We may choose to believe that there is no big deal in brokenness but encouraging one another to heal in the face of this, without allowing it to weigh us down from fulfillment and helping others concomitantly, is more than mere determination. Transcending our brokenness and frailties to demonstrating care and concern for others in their trying times is not only an act of kindness but also a divine calling.

Broken Yet Unstoppable is a mixture of painful inevitable experiences in our journey, the spiritual antidote plus the need to consistently rely on God no matter the intensity of our challenges. It reminds us that in our journey to destiny, Jesus, the Author and Finisher of our faith, brings people out of their thorns and ushers them to their place of rest and fulfillment without halting their destiny master plan.

This book is a must-read because of its practical examples and illustrations taken from the scriptures. Every page bursts with well researched and scripturally sound principles for coping with any circumstances and by not allowing these to cloud our vision for the glorious future and calling ahead. Reading this book is actually sitting and listening to divine inspirations and direction in the times of troubles. It reminds that no matter what we go through, we can still fulfill God's destiny for our life.

I have no doubts in my mind that you will find reasons to constantly read and recommend this book to others like a user's manual that catches attention in such a mesmerized reading condition because of its rich arsenal of tools for simplicity and easy understanding that is devoid of ambiguities. It is, however, a reader's guidance for lasting motivation whenever life presents a new challenge or requires an urgent solution for optimal comprehension and destiny fulfillment in our journey in life.

Rev. (Dr.) Isaac Egbewole
Lifetime Missions,
Atlanta, Georgia

Introduction

Have you ever experienced brokenness as a result of some difficult life situations, such as the death of a loved one, severe sickness, or the loss of something dear to you? Some people can attest to this. Life has some difficult moments, and we must find ways to anchor our souls when things become unbearable. Some people will anchor their hope in individuals, while others will seek to find hope and peace in the presence of Jesus. If you first find your solace with family or friends, know they can encourage and support you, but ultimately, they cannot ease your burdens or vanquish your hurt and pain. In those moments, your only trustworthy source of help is Jesus.

Let me share a brief personal story that embodies our struggles in life's most challenging moments. A few years ago, I had problems with my right rotator cuff and was in agonizing pain. I went to the doctor and discovered I had a frozen shoulder. I could not use my right arm or drive for many months. The pain was unending.

A few months later, I developed shingles as a result of the stress. The combination of these two issues was unbearable. Words cannot describe the struggles I faced waiting for them to heal. I prayed to God often, just trying to escape the pain. Although I found comfort in prayer, the pain persisted, but ultimately, I was pain-free.

I know people who will ask the 'why me' question in their painful struggles. Sometimes, this question is a whimper in these breakable moments as they battle to overcome them. I am recalling one person in particular who experienced the horrendous pain associated with having cancer. The whimper was a heartfelt cry for either quick healing or a release from their agonizing pain.

Jesus heard and responded to their cry.

Jesus understands why some of us ask the 'why me' question. He hears the groans and whimpers. He feels your pain. Remember, Hebrews 4:15 says, He is touched with the feelings of our infirmities. Jesus was not exempt from struggles; He told us we would face our own struggles.

As a result of His sacrifice on Calvary, He has provided us victory amid the pain. Life, indeed, is filled with pain, hurt, and struggles. As you face the battles, know you have an advocate with our Father in Heaven (1 John 2:1).

Isaiah 40:31 gives reassurance for the seasons of brokenness that have wearied you. It says, *but those who hope in the Lord will renew their strength. They will soar on wings like eagles; they will run and not grow weary, they will walk and not be faint. Galatians 6:9 says, and let us not grow weary of doing good, for in due season we will reap, if we do not give up.* There is a reward at the end of these hard things.

You can securely anchor your hope in Jesus.

In the midst of brokenness, you must dig deep into your soul to find strength to endure each difficult day. Maintaining your joy is the key to your strength. Nehemiah 8:10 reminds you that the joy of the Lord is your strength.

Joy is different from happiness. It is an internal, long-lasting emotion. Happiness is a temporary emotion based solely on how we feel in the moment. Happiness also depends on our daily circumstances or the people who make us happy. If things are good in our lives, then we are happy. If they are not, we become sad. Joy remains with you all through the trials and the pain. It steadies and anchors you. Joy comes from the Holy Spirit of God, who gives us gifts to enrich our lives.

If the enemy can steal your joy, he will rob you entirely of your strength.

The stories of Ruth, Naomi, and Jesus, our Kinsman-Redeemer, remind us that we can be victorious and unstoppable during great struggles and losses. Ruth and Naomi's husbands died. Naomi lost both of her children and was left without hope and home. Their stories remind us that people all around us are hurting.

You may be one of them or know someone broken yet unstoppable in their hope and confidence in Jesus.

Ruth, Naomi's daughter-in-law, refused to leave Naomi's

side as she faced the deaths of her husband and sons while in a strange land far away from home. As Naomi prepared to return to Bethlehem, her homeland, she was older, alone, bitter, and broken.

Knowing her condition, Ruth clung to her and could not be convinced to return to her own family and start a new life. Despite Ruth being broken over the loss of her husband, Naomi was even more devastated. Linking her life to Naomi's ensured Naomi would survive. Neither woman knew the future. They began each step of their journey broken yet unstoppable.

Their journey will amaze, inspire, and challenge you to rise out of brokenness, shake yourself free of pain and despair, and chart a course toward your destiny, knowing God is with you.

Romans 8:28 says, *"And we know that in all things God works for the good of those who love him, who have been called according to his purpose."*

Recently, I was at a book event and met another vendor. We began to talk, and after hearing her life story, I had to share the title of this book. Her immediate reaction was this described her journey from brokenness to becoming unstoppable.

As you read her story, you will see tenacious faith in action.

She came from a wealthy family and lived in a very exclusive neighborhood. As a student, her bus driver continually shared Jesus with her. He invited her to church, and since no one in the family would take her, the church bus picked her up each Sunday and Wednesday. After a short while, her parents became embarrassed about the unsightly bus in their community and their neighbors' reactions. They would no longer allow the bus to pick her up at home, so it began to pick her up quite a distance from the house.

Over many years, she would walk in the darkness to attend evening services and youth events. Listening to her story, I recognized she came from a broken home. She was part of a stepfamily, and that family dynamics. She had little to no support from an abusive step-parent and other family members. The remarkable thing was that despite all she endured, she had a joyful personality and used her gifts to help many students.

Earlier that day, I had stopped to hear about the student success materials she had developed. Later, I was asked to read a segment from my book, *You Can Trust Him*, as part of the event. After I read, she asked the author at the table between us if I was the one reading. Naturally, the author expressed surprise because I was standing only a few feet from her.

Why did she ask the question? She was legally blind and could only see shapes. She could not make out my features nor tell me the color of my shirt, even though I was wearing a bright blue shirt. You would not know she was blind as she spoke to people who visited her table. Remarkable! She learned her materials and presented them from memory.

This amazing woman was broken yet unstoppable. She was fearless and refused to give up on life even though she had this significant disability. After hearing her story and witnessing her tenacity, I knew I needed to share it in this book—a perfect example of how you can still triumph, no matter how broken you arc.

You can also become unstoppable because Jesus is with
you each step of the way.

Ruth and Naomi were unstoppable in their brokenness. Jesus'
body was severely broken by the beatings He endured on the
way to the cross, but He was also unstoppable. As you journey
through this book, you will discover there was a greater kinsman-redeemer than Boaz.

His name is Jesus!

This book, *Broken Yet Unstoppable*, will remind you that you
are never alone or without help. Jeremiah 20:11 says God is
with you like a mighty warrior. I encourage you to anchor your
hope in Zephaniah 3:17: *"The LORD your God is with you, the
Mighty Warrior who saves. He will take great delight in you; in
his love he will no longer rebuke you, but will rejoice over you with
singing."*

Not only is God singing over you, but He is walking with
you through each difficult day, taking you from brokenness to victory.

My prayer for you is this—as you journey through the pages of *Broken Yet Unstoppable*, God will meet with you and deposit His peace, strength, and hope into your broken heart, bringing healing and wholeness. Listen closely for His whisper—He has provided a way for your freedom from brokenness through Jesus, the unstoppable one.

Decide today to step out of brokenness and become unstoppable.

Joan E. Murray

Table of Contents

CHAPTER 1
Why Me?

*H*ave you ever asked the "Why me" questions?

Why am I going through this?
Why is God allowing this to happen to me?
Why are others doing better than me?
Why do I have to struggle so much?
Why do I have financial struggles?
Why am I always sick?
Why don't I ever get a break?

Perhaps some of you can add your own *why me* questions as you read these questions. It is a natural progression from asking these questions to asking the "What" questions. What have I done to deserve this? What is happening to me? What is God doing? What will it take to get God to move in my situation?

Throughout the Bible, people faced great struggles. Like us, they did not fully understand why life could be so difficult. I aim to answer some of the 'why me' questions by focusing this book on the lives of Naomi and Ruth.

I chose to share Ruth and Naomi's story because they faced the struggles and hardships many people in our century face. Their faith journey will inspire those of you who are determined not to allow the difficult seasons of life to stop you from maximizing your fullest potential. You, like them, are determined not to give up or settle for less than all God has for your life.

In Ruth Chapter 1, Naomi felt God had abandoned her. She probably had some of the same series of questions about her pain and struggles that were noted above. As you journey through this book, you will discover that Naomi was disappointed and discouraged by her losses.

She wanted to change her name to reflect where she was in her life's journey. She is like many of us who may have asked God' why' when our lives were filled with pain and sorrow.

Sometimes, your life may feel so out of control that you are having difficulty understanding how this could be. Naomi's life was out of control. She had lost her husband and two sons.

In that century, this meant that she lost her entire support system. When the husband died, the older son would take care of the needs of his widowed mother. Therefore, her support was now dead, and she was older with no one to provide for her needs. She was struggling to grasp what happened to her.

Can you imagine her cry, "Why God, why me?"

In the upcoming chapters, I will share how God heard and responded to Naomi's cry. You will discover how God steadied, comforted, and led her each step of the way, giving her peace in this new season of brokenness. He was her ever-present help in trouble (Psalm 46:1). He gave her a victorious outcome.

Some have wondered and even asked God where He was in their difficulties. We have discovered that life can sometimes be challenging, trying, and painful. When asking these questions, we seek answers from our only source of help, Jesus.

If you have served God for any time, you may have asked any of these questions when the journey became difficult and unbearable. The Bible is filled with many stories of how God's people struggled and questioned Him. You need to know God is perfectly okay with you asking Him questions.

He is never offended when we question our difficult circumstances. Why? He is our Father and cares about our concerns. He wants us to come to Him for the answers. Going to God deepens our relationship with Him and allows Him to speak directly to our hearts. Have you discovered that your spiritual growth does not happen on the mountaintops but in the valleys of struggles and hardships?

Think about it. Reflect on your life and examine the seasons in which you have grown the most.

What happens when we are in the valleys? We learn to lean on the only One who understands our struggles and can deliver us from the situations we face. In these valleys, we pray more, seek God more, listen more, and focus more on heavenly things. We often discover we need God more than we knew we did.

Think about a time when you were broken over a situation in your life. Did you pray and seek God more in your brokenness? Did you later reflect on how you grew during the difficulty? After receiving your deliverance, could you see that God never left your side? God uses the brokenness of our lives and gives us beauty for ashes (Isaiah 61:3).

While in the valleys, some may slip into discouragement and depression. During these times, God has encouraged you. *Hebrews 4:16 says, Therefore let us draw near with confidence to the throne of grace, so that we may receive mercy and find grace to help in time of need. 1 John 5:14 says, This is the confidence which we have before Him, that, if we ask anything according to His will, He hears us.*

You can go to God with great confidence because you belong to Him. He will hear and answer you. Whatever you ask for in accordance with His will for you, He will provide. I invite you to take God's Word and receive the help He extends to you.

God wants you to know even though the valleys are painful, you can conquer any situation. He has gone before you to smooth the crooked places (Luke 3:5).

During her journey, Ruth also had some painful seasons and experienced some deep valleys. She faced an uncertain future. By deciding to go home with Naomi instead of returning to her family, Ruth would be living among a race of people she did not fully understand.

Ruth would face hunger while also being responsible for helping her mother-in-law survive. We will explore her journey to peace and victory throughout this book.

But first, join me in looking at the desperate seasons in the lives of a few men in the Bible. Their stories will help you to see that many people faced hardships and struggles in their journeys toward a better future. They also cried out to God in their distress. They needed His help. These men had many questions for God as they struggled with brokenness.

Like Ruth and Naomi, they had to anchor their hope and trust in God and were victorious. Their stories will anchor you more securely in God's promises for your life. You will gain the victory and experience the remarkable results they achieved. You will also discover God was with them in their painful journeys. God is also with you.

Their stories will help us as we explore Ruth and Naomi's lives and journey. We will discover how to gain victory when we feel desperate enough to cry out to God for help. By looking at the lives of people in the Bible who faced tremendous hardships, we will discover some things that can help us become more than conquerors in our journeys. Let's start by studying David.

King David experienced discouragement and depression in his valleys but sought God often and found relief in prayer. David wrote the Psalms as songs of praise to God. These songs encouraged and fortified him as he faced the attacks on his life. The people sang the songs during religious events.

In these psalms, you find many prayers where David lamented before God. He sought God often for answers in his brokenness. He shows us how to cry out to God in our distress.

Let's examine the Psalms to see how he gained the victory!

In Psalm 42, David asked a lot of *why* questions. Even while asking, he still gave continual praise and thanks to God. As you show gratitude to God, you will also gain the victory. You will find solutions for your problems and have a one-on-one audience with the King of Heaven. As you connect to Him, you will learn how to soar over the obstacles you face. Jesus has the answer for everything you are currently facing.

As the deer pants for streams of water, so my soul pants for you, my God. My soul thirsts for God, for the living God. When can I go and meet with God? My tears have been my food day and night while people say to me all day long, "Where is your God?" These things I remember as I pour out my soul: how I used to go to the house of God under the protection of the Mighty One with shouts of joy and praise among the festive throng. Why, my soul, are you downcast? Why so disturbed within me? Put your hope in God, for I will yet praise him, my Savior and my God. My soul is downcast within me; therefore I will remember you from the land of the Jordan, the heights of Hermon—from Mount Mizar. Deep calls to deep in the roar of your waterfalls; all your waves and breakers have swept over me. By day the Lord directs his love, at night his song is with me—a prayer to the God

of my life. I say to God, my Rock, "Why have you forgotten me? Why must I go about mourning, oppressed by the enemy?" My bones suffer mortal agony as my foes taunt me, saying to me all day long, "Where is your God?" Why, my soul, are you downcast? Why so disturbed within me? Put your hope in God, for I will yet praise him, my Savior and my God.
  Psalm 42:1-11 (NIV)

In you, LORD my God, I put my trust. I trust in you; do not let me be put to shame, nor let my enemies triumph over me. No one who hopes in you will ever be put to shame, but shame will come on those who are treacherous without cause.
  Psalm 25:1-3 (NIV)

When the righteous cry for help, the LORD hears and delivers them out of all their troubles. The Lord is near to the broken-hearted and saves the crushed in spirit.
  Psalm 34:17-18 (NIV)

You find King David in deep distress in these Psalms and many others. He was often discouraged and dealt with depression at various times. Despite being appointed King over Israel, his struggles must have been severe because he did not immediately ascend to the throne.

First, he served King Saul, who was jealous of him and often tried to kill him. David was on the run for his life. He was homeless. At times, David was hungry. He only sometimes knew what enemy was close by. This man was chosen by God and appointed King, yet he suffered while trying to fulfill his destiny.

I can imagine him asking God the *why me* questions. He did not understand the unbearable struggles he faced. They were preparing for him to lead the multitude of Israelites. He would face the daunting task of managing a diverse group of people, each with unique challenges and complexities. All these people would have complexities he had to manage.

His struggles were the training and equipping ground. God did not bring the troubles to David because He is a good Father; instead, He allowed the devil to send the troubles because God knew David would grow and become the leader he was destined to be.

Even though you hear his pain in the scriptures, you also hear his hope in God. After every lament, David reminded himself that God was with him. David did not unplug from God when trouble came but clung more tightly to Him. We must get closer to God when we face the enemy's attacks.

David was not the only Bible hero who struggled with depression. As you continue reading, you will find that Job, Jeremiah, and Elijah also fought depression. Yet, hidden in the verses of Psalm 88, we meet a little-known man by the name of Heman, a son of Korah, who also experienced deep depression. These men faced times when it appeared God had abandoned them. Like David, they also wondered if God was available and would respond. They cried out to Him in desperation. They asked Him if He was listening. Did He hear their prayers, and would He answer them?

Job lost all ten children and his livelihood in a raid. His wife told him to curse God and die, but he refused and held on to God instead. Later, Job received a double portion for his troubles (Job 42:10). Job remained steady in his trials and gained victory.

Jeremiah had a tough kingdom assignment. He prophesied the Israelites' destruction because of their rebellion against God. Because of this, they hated him. They often tried to kill Jeremiah. He was chosen by God but rejected by those he was called to help. Ultimately, the Israelites were rejecting God and not him.

Jeremiah was lonely and unwelcome in the communities he served but did not waver in his commitment to his assignment. He wept often and was called the weeping prophet. Through all his discouragement, he pressed in closer to God. In your discouragement, push harder to get into God's presence.

The prophet Elijah faced incredible highs and lows as he served the Israelites. God's people rebelled against Him and served the false God, Baal. Elijah called for a contest against the prophets of Baal so the Israelites could decide whose God was indeed God. Elijah called fire down from heaven that consumed the sacrifice on the altar. God showed up in great power and demonstrated to His people that He alone was God. Elijah killed all the prophets of Baal.

Following this, Jezebel threatened to kill him (1 Kings 19:2). Upon hearing this threat, Elijah ran and hid. He wanted to die, and God had to comfort and reassure him. God was with him as he battled fear. God is with you when fear tries to overtake your heart.

From the lineage of Korah (Numbers 16), Heman, Dathan, and Abiram, sons of Eliab and two hundred Israelites, led a rebellion against Moses. These men were well-known community leaders and appointed council members. Yet they rebelled. They wanted the priesthood for themselves. They accused Moses of taking them away from a land flowing with milk and honey and into the desert to kill them. They also accused him of lording over them.

It's apparent that the people needed to submit more to Moses' leadership. Maybe they felt they were better leaders than Moses. Additionally, they might have felt they had better relationships with God. They may have thought they could hear God's directives better and lead His people more effectively than Moses. Something triggered them to rebel against Moses. Their decision was to their demise.

Upon hearing the complaints of these men, God opened the ground beneath them and swallowed them alive. God also sent fire and destroyed the two-hundred-fifty leaders who defied Moses' leadership. He defended Moses.

God will defend you when people try to stop you from accomplishing what He has assigned you to do.

In Psalm 88, we find the descendants of Korah. They were sad, discouraged, hurt, and confused hundreds of years after God destroyed their ancestors. Heman, who experienced great depression, pleaded with God for help. As you read this Psalm, I know that some of you may also feel as he did and, in your hurt, cried out to God. I want to assure you God hears you and will free you.

LORD, you are the God who saves me; day and night I cry out to you. May my prayer come before you; turn your ear to my cry. I am overwhelmed with troubles, and my life draws near to death. I am counted among those who go down to the pit; I am like one without strength. I am set apart with the dead, like the slain who lie in the grave, whom you remember no more, who are cut off from your care. You have put me in the lowest pit, in the darkest depths. Your wrath lies heavily on me; you have overwhelmed me with all your waves. You have taken from me my closest friends and have made me repulsive to them. I am confined and cannot escape; my eyes are dim with grief. I call to you, LORD, every day; I spread out my hands to you. Do you show your wonders to the dead? Do their spirits rise up and praise you? Is your love declared in the grave, your faithfulness in destruction? Are your wonders known in the place of darkness, or your righteous deeds in the land of oblivion? But I cry to you for help, LORD; in the morning my prayer comes before you. Why, LORD, do you reject me and hide your face from me? From my youth I have suffered and been close to death; I have borne your terrors and am in despair. Your wrath has swept over me; your terrors have destroyed me. All day long, they surround me like a flood; they have completely engulfed me. You have taken from me friend and neighbor— darkness is my closest friend.

Psalm 88:1-18 (NIV)

I shared these stories with you so you can see you are not alone.

Many people in the past and even today faced great suffering and pain. In distress, they cried out to the only One, God, who could deliver them. I wish and pray these challenging times are not upon us, but they are. We must cry out to God to intervene.

Some of you can attest to God's faithfulness because you have endured painful losses. The pandemic that recently blanked the earth has devastated many families. The pain and wounds run deep. As a result, many people are in deep depression. Some are feeling hopeless, while others have given up.

Naomi and Ruth faced hardships and grief when their husbands died. They knew pain and sorrow.

We have all heard heartbreaking stories of entire families tragically killed in accidents or by the actions of others. Many people will ask God why. Some of us choose to blame God because we reason since He is God, He should prevent these things.

We forget that humankind has been given free will. Our free

will has caused much evil to unfold on the earth. This wickedness began in the Garden of Eden when Adam and Eve used their free will and chose themselves over God. As a result of their choices, one of their sons killed his brother. They knew the depth of grief (Genesis 4:8).

Some of our choices devastate our lives and the lives of loved ones. For others, life happens. Loved ones get sick and die unexpectedly. Others died as a result of freak accidents. Jesus told us in (John 16:33) that we would have tribulation in the world but to be of good cheer because He overcame the world.

Listen, if He tells us we can be cheerful, He will help us find joy even after we have suffered horrific things. Jesus says that even when facing painful things, He is with you throughout the journey. He is your encouragement and hope during these times. He never leaves your side. Therefore, you can rejoice amid pain and hardships because He will help you overcome them.

Have you ever been in a painful season, and when you came out of it and were in a better place, you wondered how you arrived at this place? This simple answer—Jesus carried you through.

In the past two years, I have experienced the painful loss of several family members. These include my mom, dad, and brother-in-law. Their deaths have been unbearable, but God has remained constant in His faithfulness. They all died from sicknesses and diseases.

I was in the middle of a health crisis when I received the news of my mother's death. I grieved her loss as I faced major surgery. My hope and strength came from times spent in worship and prayer. Jesus walked with me through each difficult day, filling me with hope and strength as I healed and then traveled to her funeral.

His Word reminded me I would not be burned when I walked through the fiery furnaces; the flames would not set me ablaze. He was with me when sorrow tried to overwhelm me (Isaiah 43:2).

Let me encourage you. Jesus is always with you, even in your life's darkest, most difficult moments. He cannot lie and will not leave your side. He will heal and restore you.

I will share some of their journeys in this book because they will help you find hope in your journey.

Prayed Her Way into Heaven!

Since I was young, my mom, Gwendolyn (Gwen), has often woken up daily at approximately five o'clock because she started each day with prayer. The moment she opened her eyes, she began to pray. Each night, as she went to bed, she prayed. I learned from a young age that prayer is a life sustainer. Therefore, it was fitting that as she struggled with her health, she would return to what was a part of her DNA—*PRAYER*.

I called my mom, Gwen, one day to check on her. She was having great difficulty breathing. As she gasped for air, she said, "Daughter, I can't breathe." She went to the doctor, and we discovered there was fluid in her lungs. The doctor gave her some medication and sent her home. Her health did not improve. She faced her struggles and did what she has always done—*PRAYED*.

For several days after returning from the hospital, she continued struggling to breathe. One morning, she did not stop praying after her usual hour-long prayer. On this day, she prayed the entire day.

Her words, "Jesus, I am ready to come home, please take me home. I am tired of being sick. I don't want to be sick anymore. Please take me home to my rest." She continuously prayed these words all morning. At noon, my sister, Marcia, said, "Gwen, please rest yourself. You have been at this all morning."

She responded, "No, Marcia, I am ready to go home and asking Jesus to take me home." A few moments later, she began her prayer again. Her prayer continued all day until seven o'clock pm. As Marcia bathed her and prepared her for bed, she continued praying. When Marcia finished and left the room, Gwen was still praying these words.

A few minutes later, one of my brothers walked into the room and ran out, saying Gwen had died. Marcia did not believe him and called our sister, Sonia, to check on her. Gwen had indeed died. She prayed her way directly into the presence of the One she had served all her life, Jesus.

Our mother's love for Jesus and how she transitioned into heaven was a magnificent testimony to all who heard her story. She was a woman of great faith. She believed that Jesus would listen to her and grant her request.

He did not disappoint her.

Her funeral was a time of grand celebration, which was fitting. As I ministered the eulogy, I could not help but reflect on her legacy—PRAYER. Even in death, she reminded us of what happens when we have a deep, abiding relationship with Jesus—He will hear our prayers and answer us.

All who spoke about my mother spoke of her love for Jesus and deep faith. I can imagine her arrival in heaven was stellar and a grand celebration. How did my mother know that Jesus would hear and answer her? She knew Him. My mother had taken the time to cultivate a deep relationship with Him. Despite her limited education, she applied the scriptures she learned to her life. She expected when she prayed, she would have an audience with the King of Heaven.

Jesus did not disappoint her, and He won't disappoint you.

She applied Psalm 4:1 to her daily walk. *"Hear me when I call, O God of my righteousness! You have relieved me in my distress; Have mercy on me, and hear my prayer."* Do you know that each time you pray, you have an audience with God the Father, Son, and Holy Spirit? Yes, *indeed.* In your desperate cries for help, they are moved with compassion for you.

I know several people who have shared with me that their loved ones cried out to God for many weeks, months, and years, asking Him to take them home, but they did not garner the same results as my mom. *Why* they ask me.

I don't have a definitive answer, but I can conclusively say Jesus heard their prayers. My mother had a simple, childlike faith. This faith continued throughout her eighty-plus years. Her Father, my grandfather, did not believe in sending girls to school when she was growing up in Jamaica. Her husband, in the later years of her life, taught her to read. Therefore, she was simple and straightforward in her dealings with God. She just trusted Him.

Oh, how I wish I would trust Him as she did. How much farther I would be in my faith journey.

Let me encourage you don't overcomplicate God. He is your Father and hears your heartfelt, simple prayers when you pray. Daily, talk to your Daddy. He will hear and answer you. I will share the story of my dad's journey in the upcoming chapters.

King David learned in his journey with God that He is an ever-present help in times of trouble. You can be assured God is your ever-present help. David shared his battle with depression in the scriptures. He did not try to hide it. Because David exposed his struggles, he found healing.

I encourage you not to hide your depression but to reach out for help.

David wept often because, in tears, he found healing.

People are mistaken when they tell you not to weep but to be strong. Crying does not mean you are weak. It simply expresses the depth of your loss.

If weeping did not benefit our lives, God would not have given us tear ducts. Tears help to release pent-up emotions, ease the burden in our hearts, and calm our anxieties. Did you know that there are no blood vessels on the surface of the eyes? Oxygen and nutrients are transported to the surface cells by tears.

Have you ever gotten something in your eyes, dust, hair, or particle? We all have. Tears wash the eyes of these irritants. God, in His great wisdom, gave us tears for emotional healing and protection for our eyes.

Otsuka Pharmaceutical Co. LTD tells us tears keep the eyes moist and have an essential role in maintaining the functioning of the eyes.

Tears prevent infections in the eyes. Tears have a substance called lysozyme, an antibacterial that prevents invasions and diseases. Tears also contain components that heal the damage to the eye's surface. Tears do for the eyes what it does for our hearts when they are breaking—heal us.

Psalm 30:5 tells us weeping may endure for a night, but joy comes in the morning. Weep so you can heal properly and move forward into the great future God has for you.

God wants us to weep when our hearts break because He will comfort us. Weeping indicates the depths of our loss. When we cry and express our emotions through tears, rather than suppressing our feelings, we can effectively address and heal our emotional wounds with God's help.

In Deuteronomy 34:8, when Moses died, God allowed the Israelites to weep for one month, and then they had to move forward. It may be a short time to mourn any significant loss, especially our loved ones. I agree. The point is this—grieve, but don't grieve so long that you get lost in the grief. Some people never recover from their losses and stay stuck in the grieving cycle for years.

In my book, ***"Hope In Difficult Seasons,"*** I shared the grieving process and how to experience complete healing.

God told the Israelites to move forward because they could have gotten stuck in their grief and not moved into the incredible destiny He had planned for them. When your time of grieving has ended, move toward the future God has for you. You still have a purpose to fulfill despite suffering significant losses.

As you reflect on your own 'why me' questions, know that God understands. He is aware of every struggle and every tear. God knows the hard, painful seasons you have faced and might be facing now. He heard every groan when you did not have words to express the deep pain. God is not silent about you. He is listening to you. He is weeping with you.

Jesus is praying for you right now.

As we journey through the story of Naomi and Ruth, may you discover that anything and everything is possible with God. Even when your heart is breaking, keep moving forward. Your journey is not over. God will finish the great work He started in you.

Journey from Bethlehem to Moab

In the days when the judges ruled, there was a famine in the land. So a man from Bethlehem in Judah, together with his wife and two sons, went to live for a while in the country of Moab. The man's name was Elimelek, his wife's name was Naomi, and the names of his two sons were Mahlon and Kilion. They were Ephrathites from Bethlehem, Judah. And they went to Moab and lived there.
Ruth 1:1-2 (NIV)

Why did they choose Moab?

Naomi's husband, Elimelek, moved the family to Moab because they were not facing the famine plaguing his homeland of Bethlehem. He decided to move there even while being aware of the constant immorality that plagued the people in that region. Let me give you some historical background on the Moabites. It will deepen your understanding of the hardships and the losses that Naomi and her family endured. In Moab, they were away from the covering and protection of God.

The Moabites were born out of the incestuous relationship between Lot and his daughters after God rescued them from Sodom and Gomorrah (Genesis 19:37). Moab was a constant threat to the Israelites. These people represented the temptations God sought to shield the Israelites from. God wanted them to stay away from the atrocities these people committed.

The Moabites and the Israelites were in constant military conflict. The Israelites were called to live holy, set-apart lives, but they were compromised by choosing other gods over the one true living God. They compromised with the Moabites throughout the scriptures. God spoke often about Moab's unrighteousness.

In Deuteronomy 23:3, God forbids any Moabite to enter the Temple. In Judges 3, God delivered the Israelites from oppression when the King of Moab was assassinated. In Numbers 25, God saved the Israelites from being cursed by a false prophet, Balaam, yet they still turned to sexual immorality with the Moabites and committed spiritual adultery against God.

In 1 Samuel 14:47, King Saul fought against the Moabites because they were Israel's enemies. The prophet Isaiah condemned the Moabites. In 2 Samuel 8:2, King David fought against them and defeated them. Moab's chief deity was Chemosh, meaning destroyer, subduer, or fish god. This cult was introduced to the Israelites by King Solomon in (1Kings 11:7). This so-called God had a taste for blood. 2 Kings 3:27 records that human sacrifice was part of their regular rites and routines.

In Ezekiel 25, God said He would execute judgments upon Moab, and they would know He was the Lord. In Amos 2, God also said He would send fire upon Moab, and they would die amid the uproar. In Zephaniah 2:8-9 God says this about Moab:

I have heard the insults of Moab and the taunts of the Ammonites, who insulted my people and made threats against their land. Therefore, as surely as I live," declares the Lord Almighty, the God of Israel, "surely Moab will become like Sodom, the Ammonites like Gomorrah—a place of weeds and salt pits, a wasteland forever. The remnant of my people will plunder them; the survivors of my nation will inherit their land.

In 2 Chronicles 20, God delivered King Jehoshaphat from an attack by Moab and other nations. He did this by instructing the people to sing songs of worship to Him.

Let me ask the obvious question. Knowing the Moabite's history, why would Naomi's family enter this nation? God was entirely against the Israelites having any relationships with the Moabites. The reason was for their safety.

Naomi's family moved to Moab because of a famine in Bethlehem. The Word Bethlehem means the place of bread, yet famine had overtaken God's people. We know the Israelites are God's chosen people, so why did God allow the famine? The answer is simple: God's chosen people, the Israelites, constantly lived in moral decay.

They consistently strayed away from God and followed the

gods of the nations around them. They worshipped idols, which was an abomination to God. Leviticus 23:3-5 tells us, *"If you walk in my statues and keep my commandments so as to carry them out, then I shall give your rains in their season, so that the land will yield its produce and trees of the field bear their fruit."* Since the people were facing famine, it is pretty evident they did not adhere to His commandments.

God desires to prosper His people. Our financial lack is not by His design. Often, it is because of sin or wickedness.

The following scripture highlights the many blessings God wants to pour into the lives of His children. I invite you to take hold of these promises for your life.

If you fully obey the Lord your God and carefully follow all his commands, I give you today, the Lord your God will set you high above all the nations on earth. All these blessings will come on you and accompany you if you obey the Lord your God: You will be blessed in the city and blessed in the country. The fruit of your womb will be blessed, and the crops of your land and the young of your livestock—the calves of your herds and the lambs of your flocks. Your basket and your kneading trough will be blessed. You will be blessed when you come in and blessed when you go out.

The Lord will grant that the enemies who rise up against you will be defeated before you. They will come at you from one direction but flee from you in seven. The Lord will send a blessing on your barns and on everything you put your hand to. The Lord your God will bless you in the land he is giving you. The Lord will establish you as his holy people, as he promised you on oath, if you keep the commands of the Lord your God and walk in obedience to him. Then all the peoples on earth will see that you are called by the name of the Lord, and they will fear you. The Lord will grant you abundant prosperity—in the fruit of your womb, the young of your livestock and the crops of your ground—in the land he swore to your ancestors to give you. The Lord will open the heavens, the storehouse of his bounty, to send rain on your land in season and to bless all the work of your hands. You will lend to many nations but will borrow from none. The Lord will make you the head, not the tail. If you pay attention to the commands of the Lord your God that I give you this day and carefully follow them, you will always be at the top, never at the bottom. Do not turn aside from any of the commands I give you today, to the right or to the left, following other gods and serving them.
Deuteronomy 28:1-5 (KJV)

These were God's great blessings for the Israelites, yet they continually strayed and faced His judgment. He offers us these same blessings if we only do what He asks. He will keep disasters at bay. He will keep the enemy from destroying us.

Naomi's family owned much land in Bethlehem but went to Moab because of the famine and lack of crops. While there, she suffered significant losses. Her husband and sons died. Then

Naomi heard God had visited His people. This news indicated the Israelites had repented and returned to God.

Where else could they go to find food when facing hunger?

God was the only one capable of providing the necessary crops to feed them. Therefore, God again stepped in to help His wayward people when they cried out to Him. He did this, knowing the moment He blessed them and they were free from their struggles, they would once again stray from Him to follow after the nation's gods. Yet, He freed them anyway. He also does this for us. *Why*, you may ask? Because of His deep love for us.

Sin is enticing, and many people do not run away from it when they are faced with temptations. They run towards it and get deeper into ruin.

God did for the Israelites what He does for us daily. He forgives, helps, restores, and provides deliverance for us when we stray. He knows some of us will not remain committed to Him even after He frees us. Naomi's family did not stay committed to God when they faced hardship. Yet, He was committed to her and helped her in her crisis.

Naomi decided to return home since living in a strange and unrighteous nation had provided nothing of value to her life. She had stepped away from God's protection, and the results were devastating for her. As she journeyed home, God was with her and provided a friend and helper. This friend would be as valuable to her as any son who would have cared for her in old age after her husband died.

Take a journey with me and meet this amazing friend who walked with Naomi and helped her through her grieving season.

CHAPTER 2
A True Friend

Some people will tell you they have had some true, close friends. Often, we call them best friends. In this chapter, I will lay a foundation for you on how having a few close friends during seasons of brokenness can help you find your footing and gain victory in your suffering.

These friends will help you keep moving forward while reminding you that with the help of Jesus, you can become unstoppable no matter how challenging the obstacles that are in your path.

Ruth and Naomi needed each other to get to the new season God prepared for them. Because they both lost their spouses, they understood grief and being broken-hearted. They could relate to one another's grief and were ideal companions. They grew in their relationship and helped each other in their brokenness. They teach us to be more than conquerors in our painful struggles.

What makes for great friendships? It is mutual trust and respect. A true friend is honest and trustworthy. You can depend on them. They have your back. They will tell you the truth even when it is painful to hear. Instinctively, you know you can rely on them to help you.

Have you had a true friend? They are a constant source of help and encouragement to you. I have had a few close friends who have stayed by my side through each hard season. They have supported and walked with me when life's journey has been difficult. These friends have held my hands and ushered me through some challenging doors. They have reminded me that I can do anything I put my mind to and have cheered me on when I faced some of the overwhelming challenges of ministry. Their help has been invaluable. You can attest to this in your own life.

Throughout their lives, most people have had some enduring friendships that have grounded them on their journeys. These friends have done what the scriptures tell us to do. Proverb 17:17 says, *a friend loves at all times*. Proverb 18:24 says *ones who have unreliable friends soon come to ruin, but there is a friend who sticks closer than a brother*. 1 John 3:16 says, *very rarely will anyone die for a righteous person, though for a good person someone might possibly dare to die*. These scriptures depict the type of friendships we should pursue.

For the Believer, Jesus is this friend.

Some of your friends have endured with you through hard, painful seasons. They wept with you when you were broken.

They have held on to you when you needed a shoulder. They have also laughed and enjoyed rich life moments with you. They have been there in the painful seasons and the joyful-filled seasons.

Throughout our lives, God, in His infinite wisdom, has given us the kind of support we need. He has placed friends in our lives to help get us to a place of healing and wholeness. God knew painful things would happen that would cause us some breakable moments. Therefore, He sent people along the journey to help us pick up the broken pieces, find healing, and get us to the destination He had for us. In those moments, He has given us a place of shelter under the watchful eyes of dear friends.

If you have had a life-long friend, then you know how valuable they are to you and you to them. A true friend will add value to your life. There will be give-and-take in the relationship.

There is mutual giving and receiving in any healthy relationship that God ordained. It is not a healthy or valuable relationship if you do all the giving without reciprocation. We must regularly assess our relationships to ensure we are in healthy, thriving friendships.

Ruth and Naomi were friends. How deep the friendship was during Ruth's marriage to Naomi's son is unknown, but pain deepened their bond. Painful seasons in our lives can genuinely cement relationships.

The setting for the story of Ruth is Bethlehem in Judah, the birthplace of our Savior, Jesus. This story took place in the days when judges ruled. The book of Judges tells the story of Israel's history between the years of Joshua's death and the ministry of the last Judge, Samuel. The Israelites were at peace only when they served God. When they abandoned Him and worshiped idols, they endured severe consequences. When they disobeyed Him, God punished them and allowed their neighbors to conquer and rule over them. They would then return to God and ask for forgiveness. He would forgive and restore them, and they would return to their abominable ways. These unhealthy decisions were a continual pattern in Israel throughout its history. It took them a long time to learn the lessons of devotion to the One True Living God. Naomi's family was following this same pattern.

One of the main reasons we have the story of Ruth and Naomi as an example in the Bible is because Naomi's husband was disobedient to God in leaving his homeland. As they faced famine at home, he refused to surrender to God's correction of His people's waywardness. He left home. He abandoned God and went into a pagan land to get support and provision for his family. Their decision was unwise since they stepped out from under God's protection and suffered greatly as a result.

There were a total of seventeen men and one woman judge who served the Israelites during this century. They led the people to stand against their enemies and were used to uphold God's laws on Earth. Therefore, Naomi's family had leaders whom God had appointed to instruct and guide His people. Her family did not have to figure things out on their own. These judges instructed them concerning what God wanted for His people. However, like the other Israelites, they did what seemed best for them and suffered significant consequences.

As we journey through the story of Naomi and Ruth, you will see why God wanted to keep the Israelites away from the nations around them.

Now Elimelek, Naomi's husband, died, and she was left with her two sons. They married Moabite women, one named Orpah and the other Ruth. After they had lived there about ten years, both Mahlon and Kilion also died and Naomi was left without her two sons and her husband.
Ruth 1:3-5 (NIV)

Ruth's husband died.

After her devastating loss, Ruth moved forward despite the emotional pain. She refused to settle down in the situation she found herself in. Ruth had not chosen this path; it was selected for her, but she embraced it and moved on.

Is it possible Ruth did not know God intimately when she decided to go home with Naomi? Yes, it is possible, but God knew her. He was fully aware she would make herself useable to Him. As you study Ruth's life and the other stories I will present in this book, remember God knows you. He knows you will still move towards Him and your destiny in your brokenness. He will meet you and journey with you to a victorious new beginning. Keep reading and find answers to help you as you walk through the life of Ruth and Naomi.

The book of Ruth is a story of commitment, friendship, and devotion. The central message is redemption. Boaz was the kinsman redeemer who married Ruth and rescued her and Naomi from poverty. A kinsman redeemer in that century was a family member who would restore the family's name, position, lineage, and financial losses after the death of a loved one. Boaz was a type and shadow of Jesus. Jesus became our ultimate Redeemer by saying *yes* to God's will to redeem humankind. I will explore the kinsman redeemer's role more deeply in the upcoming chapters.

The purpose of the book of Ruth is to present Christ as the link to God, the Father. Jesus, our Redeemer, laid His life down to redeem us. For those who will accept and embrace Jesus' sacrifice on Calvary, you have redemption through Jesus' shed blood. As we study this book, you will discover some central truths:

God, our Redeemer, is the Holy One of Israel.
God is our Judge, and He judges and rewards us according to our faithfulness.
God is the only one who is to be worshipped. We are created for His purpose.
God is gracious, loving, and compassionate. He grants mercy to anyone who sincerely seeks Him.
God is our Redeemer/redemption. He will redeem anyone who is lost and who seeks after Him with their whole heart.

Naomi's family journey to Moab during the famine was because of a lack of faith or an unrepentant heart. They left the God-appointed land of Bethlehem and went into a land filled with idol worshipers. Again, the name Bethlehem means the house of bread.

Naomi and her family left the place of provision to go to a place they thought was bountiful. They lost more than food with this decision. In Bethlehem, God was dealing with the grievous sins of His people, the Israelites. Besides escaping the famine, Naomi's family tried to escape this reckoning with God.

As previously mentioned, the Moabite race stemmed from the incestuous union of Lot, Abraham's nephew, and his first-born daughter.

After God saved them from the destruction of Sodom, Lot's daughters got him drunk. They had sexual relationships with him because they feared they would not find husbands, get married, and bear children. It is evident that the wickedness of the people in Sodom impacted Lot's daughter's hearts and affected their lives (Genesis 19:1-38). Even though they were saved from its destruction, their hearts were affected by living amid tremendous moral decay. God tells you to guard your heart so your environment won't invade it. It's uncanny how things can sneak into our hearts and destroy our witness and destinies.

God barred the Moabites from interactions with the Israelites because they did not offer them bread and water when the hungry Israelites came out of Egypt (Deuteronomy 23:4). Later, as the Israelites made their way into Canaan, the Moabites led them into worship of the false God, Baal. The Moabites also hired Balaam, who was known as a wicked prophet, to curse the Israelites.

Although Naomi's family was facing a famine in Bethlehem, it was still God's appointed season for dealing with the waywardness of His people. God did not endorse the family moving to Moab. They missed what He planned for them and the other Israelites when they left. Think of times when you have walked away from what God asked you to do because it was too hard or you did not want to do what He asked. You may not have heard the instructions clearly. Did you find yourself in situations where you later wondered how you ended up there?

It is best not to make significant decisions when your mind is unclear due to worry and stress. Often, these decisions can have devastating effects on your life. Naomi's family was devastated because of one decision that led them out of the presence of God. They moved away from His protection, covering, and blessings. They wanted to manage their own lives and futures. They were unsuccessful.

Even as I type these statements, I am amazed at myself and others who often think we can manage without God's help. Let me shout this from the mountaintop—we cannot awaken ourselves each morning. It is not your alarm clock that awakens you each day. God awakens you daily because He still has a plan and purpose for you. God gives you a fresh start each day, just as He breathed life into Adam in the Garden of Eden. He is the only one who gives us life. Therefore, how can we expect to run our lives and determine our futures without God? We cannot do life on our own. We have been lulled to sleep by the lies of the devil.

This is the same lie the devil told Eve in the Garden of Eden. He caused her to believe God was withholding essential things from her and that she could make her own decisions without God's help. Did you know God's presence and provisions for your life are where He assigns you to be? Let me illustrate.

By day, the Lord went ahead of them in a pillar of cloud to guide them on their way and by night in a pillar of fire to give them light so they could travel by day or night. Neither the pillar of cloud by day nor the pillar of fire by night left its place in front of the people.
Exodus 13:21-22 (NIV)

Did you see it? When the Israelites left Egypt, *God's presence was with them day and night.* He was there continually. They knew when to stop or to move forward because He was their consistent guide. Canaan, the place God had sent His people, was where His presence and provisions were.

These provisions were also for Naomi's family. When they left Canaan, they left their prepared place. They walked out from under God's covering/protection and left His provisions behind.I can imagine you saying, "But Joan, there was a famine in the land, so there were no provisions for them. They would have died of starvation; that's why they left." I beg to differ. God, who allowed the famine, would have kept them alive as He did the others who remained. He was not trying to starve them to death but was using this difficult season to get the Israelites to repent and return to Him. By leaving this challenging season, Naomi's family told God they were unwilling to follow His leadership. They were not willing to go through any struggles.

Essentially, they told God, "We can manage our destinies and futures without your help." Did those words pierce your heart? They did mine. How often do we demonstrate our unwillingness to follow His lead by our actions and reactions to God's directives?

Often, we think what we are handling is manageable, so we do not need God's assistance. But we do.

Some people do not want to go through anything complicated. Unfortunately, if you live on Earth, there will be hard days. There is no escaping it. Jesus told us there would be trouble (John 16:33). He told us we could go to God for help, hope, and healing when trouble comes. Even when God allows us to endure hard times, He still watches over us. His protection is still with us during these hard seasons. If you do not feel or sense His presence, you may be offended that He has allowed the hardships. Some people are offended by God.

In Matthew 13:57, Jesus told us that the people in His hometown were offended by Him. Have you ever been offended because God did not do something you asked Him to do? I am raising my hands. Are you? I confess I get offended too often. When I pray and receive the exact appositive of what I have prayed for, sometimes I get an attitude with God. I may feel entitled to specific blessings because I am faithful in my service to Him. This is called a spirit of entitlement.

I am reminded that God and His Son owe me nothing. God's eternal love that sent Jesus to the cross of Calvary was and still is sufficient for you and me. Without His sacrifice, we would be totally loss and without hope.

Naomi's family had left God behind in Canaan. Her husband and sons died in a pagan land. She faced more incredible hardships in this land than she would have endured during the famine had they remained home. She lost everything that had value, worth, and significance to her. When they faced the famine, they assumed it would devastate their lives. Naomi and her family were not aware that without God's constant protection over them, the enemy would destroy their lives in more significant ways.

Think about times when you thought you were doing the right thing, only to discover later it was the wrong move. Yep, I have done the very same thing. At the time Naomi's family left Judah, God had allowed the famine in the land as a chastisement or punishment for the Israelite's sins. The famine was a call to repentance. Therefore, when Naomi and her family went to Moab, they sinned through disobedience because they did not stay in Bethlehem and face their punishment. Although the family escaped one difficulty, ten years later, Naomi faced greater ones. More significant challenges resulted in a deeper level of pain lasting throughout the remainder of her life.

A Committed Friend

Commit to the Lord whatever you do, and he will establish your plans. Proverbs 16:3 (NIV)

Ruth demonstrated a level of commitment to Naomi that we rarely see today. Commitment speaks of giving your word and understanding; it is a pledge you make. It is as binding as a contract. It means pledging to serve people who expect you to keep your word and do as you say. Ruth took custody of Naomi and committed to not leaving her. She provided for all Naomi's needs. Ruth clung tightly to Naomi in her despair. Therefore, Ruth was bound by her words and integrity, the glue that held the friendship together.

Ruth was a devoted daughter-in-law. She became similar to a son to Naomi because she provided for her, as was the custom for sons to provide for their widowed mothers in that century.

Her statements of commitment were:

- She would go wherever Naomi went.
- Naomi's people would become her people, and most importantly,
- Naomi's God would become her God.

Ruth renounced her idol gods and embraced the one true living God. Naomi and her family influenced Ruth with their godly beliefs. Embracing their beliefs made Ruth one of God's children, allowing her to take advantage of all the rights and privileges of belonging to God. This transformation brought abundant blessings and favor for Ruth.

Ruth represents what happens to Believers in Jesus Christ. When we first encounter Jesus, we are lost and without hope. When we invite Him into our hearts, we go from being lost to having an eternal relationship with Him. He becomes our Father.

We each choose and take a step of faith to receive Jesus as our personal Savior and Lord. We then live our lives in faith and trust His guidance. Ultimately, we receive the reward for our faith. The reward for faith is a relationship with Jesus, the Son of God.

Through prayer and time reading the scriptures, we experience His presence daily. He helps us to make the right decisions. He leads us along the best pathway for our lives. He fills us with hope and confidence for the future because He guides our lives and reminds us that we are loved.

———

Having entered a relationship with God, Ruth was
rewarded for her faith.

———

Trusting in Jesus leads to a rich and fulfilling life. I am not saying we will not encounter difficulties or challenges in this new relationship, but we have an anchor during these times. Jesus will stabilize us and keep us moving forward in the storms.

Ruth's level of commitment garnered her great success. She succeeded because she was committed to serving Naomi, not just pursuing her interests. This commitment was pure and unselfish. It demonstrated her deep love and devotion to her mother-in-law. She was greatly rewarded for her acts of service. When we give of ourselves in this way, it is impossible not to experience God's blessings.

Let's look deeper at commitment to see the depth of Ruth's sacrifice. Commitment means to do what you say.

Commitment means being entrusted with responsibilities and handling them with integrity.

Commitment is making time when you may wonder where to find the time. Commitment contains the power to change people's lives. It helps to develop and refine our character. It is one of the most significant responsibilities of our lives. Why? It transforms our words and the promises given into reality. This reality affects those around us. People often give us their word, but some need to follow through.

Think about your level of commitment to God. Do you often follow through on what you have promised Him? If yes, you may have discovered that you are more profoundly committed to other things due to your commitment to Him.

When we are committed to God, that overflows into other areas of our lives. When we lack commitment toward Him, we may also lack commitment to others. I want you to see that your commitment to God will help you be more committed to the people in your life. If we struggle to commit to Him, we will struggle to commit to others.

What keeps us from fulfilling our commitments? Indeed, crises in our lives whether they are relational, financial, or within the family unit. The enemy sends these things to reroute us from our commitment to God and others. Crises can break our focus and can keep us off-balance. Ruth's commitment to Naomi speaks clearly to our hearts about what it takes to give sacrificially. She exemplified what Jesus said and did—laying down His life to serve others. Ruth gave up her entire life for her friend but found a more prosperous, more fulfilling life in God. She held tightly to Naomi in her seasons of loss. Ruth came through during the hard, painful times and nourished Naomi's thirsty soul. True friendships nourish our lives in the dry seasons and keep us from giving up.

In Exodus 17, the Amalekites attacked the Israelites. Moses, Aaron, and Hur went to the top of the hill to view the battle. While there, Moses extended his arms as the battle raged. As long as his arms remained extended, the Israelites prevailed. When his arms became tired, and he lowered them, the Amalekites prevailed. Aaron and Hur provided a stone for Moses to sit on. They each held one of his arms up, allowing Joshua and the Israeli army to be victorious. Do you see it? We all need help in the journeys of life. This help is invaluable to our success. Surrounding yourself with people who understand your challenges and are willing to lend a helping hand eases your burdens and loads.

Moses needed help to ensure the Israelites' victory. Have you had friends who held your hands when you were weary? They helped you not to lose sight of God in the struggles. They encouraged and supported you when you wondered if you would overcome the hardships. Without proper support and encouragement, many people will lose their way or be unsuccessful in their struggles.

Ruth's help boosted Naomi's faith. It influenced her when her faith was falling. It helped her regain her footing and comfort her wounded soul. God positioned people next to Moses to help him when he needed it. He did the same for Naomi. He is faithful in the hard seasons. God will also do this for you. Perhaps He already has.

Think of the times your friends have held you up when you felt there was no point in continuing. How about times when you wondered if life was worth living? Because of their hardships, some may have thought it would be better if they did not exist. As a result of their pain, so many people in society have died by suicide and left their loved ones devastated.

Often, the devil whispers in people's ears, 'No one will miss them if they take the ultimate step of ending their lives.' John 10:10 says the thief comes only to steal, kill, and destroy, but Jesus came so we may have life and have it to the full. True friends help to make your life whole. They keep you steady on your path to a brighter tomorrow.

Commitment is the transforming power behind your word. It can alter someone's life and destiny. Truly, commitment speaks of our character and intentions. When we commit, it speaks loudly of who we are. It says I am here. I am not leaving. I love you enough to keep you afloat until you can confidently rerun your race.

I encourage you to use your commitment to others to change the situations all around you.

Ponder these questions:

How committed are you to your friendships?
Can your friends count on you at any time?
Do your friends add value to your life?
Are your friendships draining the life out of you?
Are they propelling you to greater success?
Do they influence you toward the greater good?
Do they nourish your soul?
Are you one of those who are genuinely committed?

Your commitment is your pledge that you will come through on your word. It is steadfastness. It keeps you from being easily moved from the stance you have taken. God will reward you for your commitment.

The Friend Who Stayed

But Ruth said: "Entreat me not to leave you, or to turn back from following after you; for wherever you go, I will go; and wherever you lodge, I will lodge;

Your people shall be my people, and your God, my God. Where you die, I will die, and there will I be buried. The Lord do so to me, and more also, if anything but death parts you and me."

When she saw that she was determined to go with her, she stopped speaking to her.
   Ruth 1:16-18 (NKJV)

We read earlier that after the death of Elimelek, his sons married Moabite women named Orpah and Ruth. Both sons died, leaving two more widows. Naomi was no longer alone in her painful season of widowhood. After these events, Naomi was ready to return home. She was broken, empty, poor, and suffering. Yet, she encouraged her daughters-in-law to return to their own families. If they followed her instructions, she would be entirely alone. She was older, without family, and had no financial support. Orpah listened and returned to her family, but Ruth refused to leave Naomi's side. It is evident from this beautiful passage that God, knowing the future events, had already begun a deep work in Ruth's heart. This allowed her to leave her homeland and all she knew for Naomi.

What a beautiful picture of Jesus giving His life in exchange for ours.

Let me propose something more significant than Ruth's devotion to Naomi. Even though she was unaware of it, God had a great destiny for Ruth. God has a great destiny for you. We are often unaware of the future He has planned for us. A future filled with abundant blessings (Jeremiah 29:11). Some people have not discovered this because they have not spent time with Jesus, who knows all the plans for their futures.

A hindrance to discovering God's plans is we often have our plans and futures mapped out. This makes it hard for us to hear God and change course.

Can you bear witness to this? I can. At no time in my college years did I ever think I would be in ministry or even become an author. Desperate, I sought God one day because my life seemed mediocre. God heard me, and because I was willing, ready, and obedient, He began to open my eyes and ears to His plans for my future. I shared this story in my book, *Called and Chosen for Destiny*.

God had set the stage to get Ruth to the great future He prepared for her. All she had to do was listen, hear, and obey His still small voice. God often whispers things to us, giving us directions for our future. Are you listening to your instructions? Ruth instinctively knew she could not leave Naomi's side and let her return home alone. Saying yes ensured she did not miss the phenomenal destiny God mapped out for her.

Do not miss the great things God wants to do in and through you. His plan for you is filled with great abundance.

Because Ruth insisted on going with her, Naomi consented. Let me ask this—do you think God only had a plan for Ruth's life? Is it possible He also had a plan for Orpah, the other daughter-in-law? Romans 2:11 says God is no respecter of person. God values each person equally. He is not partial in His love for us. He loves us equally, and if you were the only person on planet Earth, He would have still sent Jesus to die just for you because you are special to Him. I believe if Orpah had chosen to go with them, we may still be hearing about her today. Remember, God wants all His creations to be saved and become His chosen people.

As a result of Naomi's and her husband's choices, she experienced the pain of disappointment, loss, death, and grief, but ultimately renewal. Choosing disobedience leads to enduring challenges and more hardships, much like Naomi experienced. Once we repent and return to God, we can often return to the beginning and start again. God can and will renew and restore you as you restart your journey in obedience.

Once back home, Naomi rediscovered this was where God's protection was for her all along. Naomi was renewed and restored. Please hear me—God did not leave Naomi; she left Him. He was right where she left Him, awaiting her return. God did not scold or show disappointment for her lack of foresight as she faced her struggles.

God will not show disappointment in you when you make wrong choices. He is ready to receive and restore you when you return to Him.

Upon arrival, the people welcomed Naomi home. God set the stage to help her readjust. Naomi could not see God at work, so she wanted to change her name to Mara, which means bitter. She felt God had dealt her a bitter blow. Notice that Naomi blamed God for her hardships and pain. It appears she did not consider her family's choices led her down this road.

How often do we blame God when our decisions cause us suffering? God is a good Father who truly desires to safeguard us from hurt and pain. Yet, He knows we will make decisions that will make our lives difficult. He awaits us with the comfort of the Holy Spirit and answers when we seek Him.

Our choices affect our lives sometimes in obvious ways but at other times in subtle ways. We miss promotions, divine connections, and divine appointments because our choices move us out from under the protection of God, our Father.

Our choices also cause us to miss hearing His clear directions for our future.

After returning home, Naomi experienced the difference between being in God's presence and under His protection versus when she was away from Him. We will explore this in the upcoming chapters.

Naomi found a friend in Ruth. This friendship provided her with companionship and ensured a future filled with blessings and provisions for her life. This plan was not Ruth's plan but God's. He used Ruth to accomplish what He wanted to be done in Naomi's life.

I am reminded of Romans 8:28, which says, "*And we know that all things work together for good to those who love God, to those who are the called according to His purpose.*"

Naomi's journey and her friendship with Ruth were just the beginning. God was about to make the latter years of her life more remarkable than the former (Job 8:7).

Friends are needed to help heal our broken hearts and restore our lives. You may be experiencing brokenness, as did Naomi and Ruth. Still, you can be unstoppable as you anchor your hope securely in Jesus and allow your friends to help you overcome the struggles and gain victory.

As you journey through Ruth's and Naomi's stories, you will uncover how God helps us in our weaknesses and brokenness.

CHAPTER 3

The Journey Is Hard

This title is challenging to hear and absorb. *Why?* Many of us are already experiencing hard times. We do not want to hear about additional hard times, but stick with me because you will glean things designed to help you be an overcomer. As you overcome, you can direct others to the One who saves, heals, and delivers —JESUS.

As I reflected on the journey of Ruth and Naomi, I concluded that sharing about the hardness of their journey was necessary so you could grasp the depth of their struggles. Their journey is an excellent reminder if you are facing your hard season. Although the journey is challenging, you will reap a harvest of blessings on the other side of it. Remember, God is no respecter of persons, and just as He helped Ruth and Naomi, He will also help you.

Many of us can attest to some arduous journeys as we pursued the destinies God had for us. For some, life has been difficult due to health challenges, financial and family struggles, and many other complicated things they have faced. We all know people who have endured some painful seasons.

We often encouraged and supported them but could not help them in other ways because we were also in seasons of hardships. I can think of times when friends have encouraged me during unemployment and when I was struggling financially. There are also times when I have supported, encouraged, and prayed for these friends and other people I have encountered while ministering. I am sure you can attest to being helped and providing help and support to those in your inner circle. It is a gift from God to have loving, supportive people in our lives during challenging seasons.

I can recall numerous times I have prayed for people during church services or on the phone while going through my difficulties. Their pain was so real it was almost tangible. I am thinking of one particular lady—her pain was so deep that as I prayed, all she could do was lay her head on my shoulder and sob.

If you are anything like me, you have asked why life is so hard and painful. Have you discovered the reasons yet?

Let's explore some reasons together. We truly live in a fallen world. From the time the devil was kicked out of heaven (Luke 10:18) until today, humankind has struggled with sin, making for complex, difficult times.

It began in the Garden of Eden when Adam and Eve sinned. Their sin affected their children, causing one son to kill the other out of jealousy and envy. Their disobedience caused us to be born sinful (Psalm 51:5). With this nature and free will, we have the propensity to choose wrong over right more often than not.

After they sinned, Adam had to work hard, tilling the ground to produce food for them. He had not experienced this before. Eve endured tremendous pain during childbirth —hardships.

As you think of the family dynamics today, the husbands and wives work hard to sustain their families. Others work hard to maintain their lifestyles. Many mothers have it especially hard since they are often responsible for the children and the home, all while working to contribute financially to sustain the family.

According to the 2021 U.S. Census Bureau, out of approximately eleven million single-parent families with children under 18, nearly eighty percent are headed by single mothers. For those of you who are single parents and for those of us who know single parents, we have heard of the tremendous struggles and hardships you face. Many are exhausted from all their responsibilities, yet they keep persevering.

These challenges are the legacy of Adam and Eve, our fore-parents. Their sin of disobedience caused a huge ripple effect in families. When Adam allowed the devil to talk to Eve and did not dissuade her from eating the forbidden fruit but joined in this disobedience, something broke within the family structure.

The man, the leader God appointed, did not lead, and we see the results of this lack of leadership in many families. This lack of leadership is also seen in many single-parent families that dot our landscape and worldwide. I have many friends who are single parents and have counseled many of them over the years. They have shared their unbelievable struggles with me, and I will highlight a few here.

A couple of my friends shared their struggles of being single moms. They worked hard, were weary, and often did not have food for themselves after feeding their kids. They sometimes wondered how they would make it since they had to be both father and mother. They were the primary providers of the family's financial needs.

If they received child support, it was never enough to meet their everyday needs. These parents were entirely on their own in figuring out how to keep the children healthy and thriving. One mom shared that as the daily struggles unfolded, she contemplated suicide. With God's help, she did not give up. She might have been broken, but she was unstoppable.

What tremendous hardships for these mothers and fathers.

Many were devastated because this was not how they planned their futures. None had planned to become single parents. None planned on being divorced. They took what life handed them and did the best they could with it. They *persevered*.

Some succeeded in raising amazing kids. Others are still struggling today because of how the home environment affected their children—some are deceased. Other children are either in jail or barely surviving life. So many single parents are still brokenhearted and seeking solace in God. These challenges trace their roots back to the events in the Garden of Eden when Adam and Eve turned away from God's design and succumbed to the deceitful whispers of the enemy.

Beyond what Adam and Eve did, we have also made choices that have caused us hardships. When making these decisions, we seldom count the cost to our lives. We assume all will go well.

Others might have been aware of the consequences but decided to proceed because it was what they wanted to do.

When we face the hard things, we generally look for someone to blame. Who gets the most blame—GOD? The Bible tells us that God is not the author of confusion (1 Corinthians 14:33). He does *not cause* the hard things in your life. He is a good and faithful Father who watches over you, providing help and a way through each painful decision.

Like Adam and Eve, who blamed one another and the serpent, we look for others to blame so we don't have to own our actions. Whether or not you accept responsibility, you are the one who will have to walk the challenging journey to your freedom.

Jesus offers you help.

All things work together for good for those who love the Lord and are called according to his purpose.
Romans 8:28 (NIV)

The LORD is a refuge for the oppressed, a stronghold in times of trouble. Those who know your name trust in you, for you, LORD, have never forsaken those who seek you.
Psalm 9:9-10 (NIV).

Cast all your anxiety on him because he cares for you. Be alert and of sober mind. Your enemy the devil prowls around like a

roaring lion looking for someone to devour. Resist him, standing firm in the faith, because you know that the family of believers throughout the world is undergoing the same kind of sufferings.
1 Peter 5:7-9 (NIV)

The concurrent theme you see in these scriptures are:

God is working in your favor because He loves you.
He is working out every wrong decision for your good.
He is a refuge when you are overloaded in your struggles.
He is your safe place during times of trouble.
He sees your anxiety and will do something about it.
He can and will alert you of attacks from the enemy.
You can release your cares to Him because He will care for them and you.
He has never forsaken you, and He never will.
You can depend on God to see you through.

The devil brings troubles and hardships to your life, but God will use it for your advancement. He will not let the enemy win. God will not disappoint you when you anchor your trust securely in Him.

As we take an in-depth look at Ruth and Naomi's journey, you will see that they struggled just as people of today are struggling. They were left without the means to support themselves and probably anxious and fearful for their futures. They had to trust the same God Naomi believed dealt her a painful blow. Naomi was bitter and struggling. Ruth was journeying with Naomi and caring for her while trusting that Naomi's God would rescue and provide for them.

The Journey Begins

When Naomi heard in Moab that the Lord had come to the aid of his people by providing food for them, she and her daughters-in-law prepared to return home from there.
Ruth 1:6 (NIV)

Words of God's faithfulness to His people reached Ruth and Naomi in Moab. God ensured Naomi received the message of His provisions so she would return to her homeland. Even though Naomi felt as if her life was over, God was not done with her yet.

There are times in our lives when things are so excruciating and challenging that we may think this is the end. It is never the end in God's eyes. God knows we are in struggles that are way beyond our ability to deal with. He sees and knows your trials and tribulations and what you are made of. God knows you have grit and will make it through with His help and encouragement. Naomi was exhausted from life. She was worn down. She had no hope of a better tomorrow, but God did. If your tomorrow does not look promising, it does not mean God cannot turn it around for you. I say this often, "God sees what we cannot see and is way ahead of us with His plans for our future. We must *TRUST* Him." In my book, **You Can Trust Him,** I shared how God proved His trustworthiness in the lives of many modern-day men, women, and many others in the Bible. He was with them through all of the challenging seasons and ensured they were victorious as they trusted Him for their victory.

Let me ask this question. Did Naomi *see* the provisions while living in Moab or did she only hear that God provided? She heard. She did not see them. Naomi and Ruth had to believe the report and move in faith towards God's provision. We also hear reports of God's faithfulness and must trust that He will be faithful to us. Naomi discovered that believing was better than doubting. She stepped out in faith, expecting a better outcome than the one she was facing. Naomi may have felt bitterness towards God but knew He was faithful nonetheless. She had seen His faithfulness throughout her life.

Think of the many times in the scriptures when God cared for widows. She was a widow and knew God would take care of her. She did not know how, but she had enough faith to believe. Taking the first step in her difficult journey would get her on the right path to a better tomorrow. When Naomi left home, she was blessed because her family and friends surrounded her. As she returned, she felt empty because of her losses and had only one daughter-in-law who was willing to lay down her life to follow her into this painful season.

Let's explore these steps that would deposit her back in her homeland and into a new beginning and a new season of life.

The journey from Moab to Bethlehem was approximately

fifty miles over a mountainous terrain. It took seven to ten days to walk the distance. This was a challenging trek. Think about your journey and walk with me in Naomi's shoes.

Imagine the regrets and questions she must have had: If we had stayed home in Bethlehem, my life would be better. Was God punishing me because I left Him? My husband was the decision-maker, and I followed his lead. Why am I the only one in the family who survived? Why did God not take me? What will my friends say when they see me broken and without family? What if I am rejected after being gone so long? What if I am judged for missing God's plans?

Does anyone else ever have these thoughts or questions? I am shouting, "YES." The devil does so much damage to our minds when we are experiencing broken because of our choices. While he is yelling that you caused this, God is saying He will make the enemy pay for all the pain you are enduring. God will pick you up from the ashes and restore beauty to your life. He is in the restoration business, and Naomi is about to discover this firsthand.

Naomi's steps were difficult and challenging, but each led her to a brighter future. God showed her His love, mercy, and compassion. He valued her and showed her she was still needed. Her purpose on earth was incomplete, even though she could not see it. God can use any broken vessel for His greater good.

Have you lost loved ones? If you have lost a parent, spouse, or child, you might feel as if your life is over. You may not think there is any reason to go on. Some feel they no longer have anything else to contribute.

I have heard these words from my own family. I have listened to them from grieving parents and spouses. I want to shout this from the mountaintop—if you are still here, God is not finished with you yet. He still has an excellent plan for your future.

Do you know God is the only one you cannot ultimately live without? Think about it. In the wedding vow, we hear, "Until death do us part." These words signify the closest person in your life will die and transition into heaven if they are Christians. The death of a spouse is one of the most painful separations that many people endure. I have, however, seen many people who, after losing a spouse, remarry and are just as happy as before.

The only person you and I cannot live without is JESUS. If He ever leaves us, we would indeed be without hope. That is why the Bible repeatedly tells us that God will NEVER leave or forsake us. He can't. It is not possible.

We need Him for the very breath we breathe. We need Him to watch over our every move to keep us from harm. We need God to navigate through life. We need Him to shelter us from the storms that rage around us. We need Him to quiet our anxious souls. We NEED HIM. Do you see it? We CANNOT live without Him. We can and will move forward after a significant personal loss, but without Jesus, we are eternally lost. He is the only One; if He ever leaves us, we will be truly lost and devastated. Aren't you glad He promised never to leave you (Hebrews 13:5)?

Naomi and Ruth were walking this journey after losing their spouses. Even though their spouses were now absent, the women soon discovered God was with them each painful step of the way. He would be their constant source of help and strength. He would guide, instruct, help, provide, and deliver them safely to the other side of eternity when it was their time to meet Him in heaven.

I Won't Leave You

Let's pick the story of Ruth and Naomi back up again. Naomi urged Ruth to return to her own people while Naomi traveled to Bethlehem alone.

But Ruth replied, "Don't urge me to leave you or to turn back from you. Where you go, I will go, and where you stay, I will stay. Your people will be my people, and your God my God. Where you die, I will die, and there I will be buried. May the Lord deal with me, be it ever so severely, if even death separates you and me." When Naomi realized that Ruth was determined to go with her, she stopped urging her.

Ruth 1:16-18 (NIV)

As you read this passage, what a perfect description of God's unrelenting love for us! Like Ruth, God never leaves us. He is steadfast in His love toward us even when we step outside His perfect plan.

Ruth was discovering Naomi's God to be an ever-present help in times of trouble (Psalm 46:1). As a gentile woman, she probably had not yet discovered the depth of God's compassion for those who are hurting. In her brokenness and during this painful season, a comforter in Israel was ready to help her find hope and healing—God.

The scripture does not tell us how long Ruth was married to Mahlon. We read that after living in Moab for ten years, Mahlon and his brother Kilion died.

Let's explore the meaning of their names for a few minutes. Mahlon means 'sick or sickly'. Kilion means 'pining or wasting away.' Are you wondering why these parents would give their children such dreadful names? I am.

The Israelites traditionally gave their children names that reflected their futures. Therefore, each time you said their names, it spoke their destinies over them. Remember, in Genesis 32, God changed Jacob's name, which meant trickster and supplanter, to Israel, meaning prince of God or ruled by God. This name change was to speak into existence the destiny for which he was born. With the name Jacob, he lived a life that did not reflect who he was created to be, so God did something about it—He changed his name. You will find name changes throughout the Bible. With names such as Mahlon and Kilion, is it any wonder they both died early? Daily calling them 'sick and wasting away' did not produce life in them. Each time their names were spoken, they heard disease and death.

Even though Ruth was grieving the loss of her husband, she set her hurts aside to take care of her mother-in-law. From the above scripture, you see a deep bond, a special love between Naomi and her daughters-in-law. They clung to her, wept over her, and genuinely did not want to leave her side. Even though Orpah returned to her family, Ruth stayed. It is fair to conclude that Naomi was a great example to them.

Ruth began the journey of a lifetime with Naomi. She had no idea what she was undertaking. She left her family and friends, familiar surroundings, traditions, and all she knew to follow Naomi into the unknown. I am reminded of Abraham in Genesis 12 when God told him to leave his family and familiar surroundings, and he obeyed. Abraham did not know where God was leading him, but he began a journey that would change him forever. He was ushered into an amazing destiny and became the father of many nations.

You are a part of his lineage.

As a Gentile, an outsider, Ruth was stepping into a situation that was not the norm for the Israeli race. In Deuteronomy 7, the Israelites were told not to intermarry with other races. Was God banning interracial marriages? No. When God gave the Israelites this commandment, they were about to enter Canaan, their Promised Land.

God was warning them not to marry the people in that territory. Why? They were idol worshipers who practiced temple prostitution, adultery, homosexuality, incest, murder, bestiality, gang rape, and child sacrifice. They were an evil race. By marrying these people, the Israelites would turn away from following God to committing these practices.

Remember how Solomon married seven hundred women and had three hundred concubines (1 Kings 11:3)? They turned his heart away from God. God was attempting to keep the Israelites from straying into a similar situation.

Sometimes, as Christians, we feel like we are the influencers. Have you noticed that it is often easier for the world to entice Christians away from God instead of us influencing them to follow Him? God knew this would happen should His people marry into this group. Do you think they listened to Him? No. They did what they wanted and then suffered the consequences. Although Ruth's lineage was filled with atrocities, she had a different spirit.

As Ruth began the journey, I am sure she was filled with trepidation. What would she encounter? Would these people welcome her? Would she suffer harm? Would she struggle to survive? How would she provide for herself and Naomi, who was too old to remarry? For a moment, let's walk in Ruth's shoes. She was probably nervous, anxious, worried, fearful, and wondering what the future held.

Do you feel like that at times? The uncertainty all around you causes uneasiness and anxiety. None of us know what tomorrow will bring. We see chaos all around us. I know many parents who are raising their grandchildren due to the untimely death of their children or because some of their children are caught in addictions. Life hands us many unexpected things to handle. We have to choose the path we will take.

Some people get overwhelmed when faced with these challenges, which is normal. Others accept the assignments and make the best of it. Still, others may wonder how this could happen to them because it was not a part of their life plans or goals. As we face these challenges, we may not know what tomorrow holds, but we know God is already in our tomorrow, and He holds it together.

Think about some of the unexpected things you have endured or might be currently enduring. These changes have left you wondering how you ended up in these difficult times. You may not be grieving the loss of a loved one, but maybe the loss of your freedom. How about the loss of your retirement and the rest you hoped to enjoy during these latter years? Have these things changed your life drastically? Listen to this story. You might identify with it or know someone who is.

My staff and I recently conducted an outreach event in a low-cost housing apartment complex. A gentleman in his mid to late seventies was doing laundry at the laundry mat in the complex. One of his neighbors asked if he was bringing his grandchildren to get backpacks and school supplies. He went and gathered them. What was astounding was that there were approximately eight of them as they appeared.

Just before I shared the message with the community, I looked into his face and was prompted to ask if the children were visiting or if they lived with him. I was stunned when he affirmed they all lived with him. It was hard for me to begin the message after hearing this. I felt his burden and was so sorry that at this late stage in his life, when he should be enjoying retirement, he had such a huge load to carry.

He had raised his children and should have been enjoying the latter years of his life, but he was once again raising children. His grandchildren were between six and ten years old. They all lived in his small apartment home. Even as I type his story, I am still led to pray for him. My prayer for him and other parents is that God would rescue their children who are still alive but are caught in the vicious cycle of addictions so they can take on the responsibilities for their children.

At times, life can be filled with hardships. This gentleman was experiencing it. Some of you are dealing with that now. Your encouragement today is just as God was with Ruth in her grief, lack, hunger, and pain; He is also with you. Anchor your hope steadfastly in this.

I know! I sometimes battle to hold onto this belief when facing pain or lack, but our *God can be trusted*. Keep repeating this to yourself and wait for the manifestation of His goodness to you.

Ruth spoke these profound words to Naomi, and God honored her. *Where you go, I will go, and where you stay, I will stay. Your people will be my people, and your God my God. Where you die, I will die, and there I will be buried. May the Lord deal with me, be it ever so severely, if even death separates you and me."*

Ruth did not simply make a commitment, which is so often easily broken. She made a covenant with Naomi and God about the remaining days of her life. A covenant is far superior to a commitment. It is much easier to break a commitment than a covenant. Biblical covenants are binding agreements or legal contracts that are sealed between two or more people. The root meaning of covenant is 'to cut," and in biblical times, covenants carried weight and were often cut or sealed in blood, (Genesis 17:1-2).

Ruth would give her all in service to Naomi and her God. God heard her pledge and began to move on her behalf. Before Ruth ever reached Naomi's homeland, God had spread the word about her character, love, devotion, and commitment to Naomi. He set the stage for the abundant blessings He would pour into her life.

God is looking for people like Ruth, who will do what they say. I said it before, but it bears repeating. Ruth laid down her life for Naomi as Jesus would, hundreds of years later. He laid down His life for humankind.

Ruth's words to Naomi were as steadfast as God's promises to the Israelites throughout their journey to the Promised Land. He led them each step of the way. He was their cloud by day and a pillar of fire by night. When He moved, they moved with

Him. When He stopped, they did the same. He was their shelter from the day's heat and guiding light at night.

Ruth's words reassured Naomi. Declaring she would live, die, and be buried wherever Naomi was, this said to Naomi that Ruth would never leave her side. Can you see the absolute comfort in those words for a broken and despairing woman?

She would have a constant companion throughout her latter days.

Can you hear the voice of God speaking these words of comfort to Naomi's wounded heart? God knew how to settle her anxious soul. He knows how to calm you when anxiety tries to steal your breath. When worry and fear beset your life, Jesus whispers He is with you, ready to bring hope, help, and healing. When the journey is painful and exhausting, lean into the comfort of the Holy Spirit so you can catch the next breath and find the necessary strength to take the next step. Jesus knows what's in you, and even when you feel that you cannot make it, He helps you find the strength to continue putting one foot in front of the other.

Naomi and Ruth found this strength as they began the journey. Their strength came from the Lord. Your strength also comes from the Lord. Tap into it today.

I close this chapter with a story of one of my co-laborers in the gospel, Phyllis. She is an excellent example who keeps pushing through hardships despite struggling with pain and brokenness. She has demonstrated such great strength even while physically suffering.

Throughout our years of working together, she seldom spoke of the physical pain she endured from an accident years prior. I was only able to tell she was in severe pain by looking at her face. She is such a trooper and consistently pushes through the hard seasons in her life. Even with all she has endured over the seventeen years I have known and served with her, she was recently diagnosed with Parkinson's disease.

We noticed she kept falling for no apparent reason, and it took a while for us to discover what was wrong with her. She had spent many days in and out of the emergency room because of these falls and was often in constant pain. She and I would pray through the pain. As we prayed, often with tears in her voice, she still thanked God. She reminds Him constantly that she trusts Him even though she does not understand this painful season.

I will be the first to tell you that it is heartbreaking to watch those you love suffer, and at times, you have to resist the urge to ask Jesus why He does not heal the instant you pray. I must admit that I don't always succeed in not asking the question.

I often return to this—I trust you, Jesus, no matter what I face.

In a recent conversation with Phyllis, I was again reminded of her tenacity. She was in great pain but was pressing through.

She was hurting and crying but refused to stop trying and believing. So many people give up when the journey gets hard.

I have sometimes been tempted to give up because the stress and the load are too hard to bear. Without knowing it, Phyllis reminds me each time I talk with her that I must also be optimistic. Since she can still be hopeful with all the challenges in her life, so should I. She finds her strength in the promises of Jesus.

Phyllis' struggles with Parkinson's disease and her daily hardships remind us of the struggles and hardships of Ruth and Naomi. They, too, had to embrace their painful season and keep moving. They had to trust God each step of the way. They did not know what each new day would bring but trusted the One who controlled each day. You can trust Jesus with each of your difficult days. He will walk with you each step of the way as He did with Ruth and Naomi and is daily walking with Phyllis.

Naomi and Ruth needed courage as they began the journey. They found it deep in their souls. They knew God would see them through. Your courage also comes from the Lord. He will lead and guide you.

Remember, just like Ruth, Naomi, Phyllis, and many others in the Bible, you can still be unstoppable even when you don't understand why the journey is so difficult. You have help to get you to the end of the journey and into your promised land—Jesus.

CHAPTER 4

Divine Favor

One of the things we know about God is He has a divine nature. His laws are divine. He gives divine direction to us. When we think of the word divine, it speaks of profound insight. It means holy, sacred, and spiritual. The word divine is used to describe Jesus as the Divine Savior. The Greek word for divine is 'Theias,' the adjective for divinity. Divine truly defines God as the Supreme Being. He is a perfect being. He is omnipresent, omniscient, and omnipotent.

You may have heard these words, but let me help you understand their meaning concerning who God is. Omnipresent means God is everywhere. Omniscience means He knows everything. Omnipotent means He has unlimited power and can do anything.

With these definitions in mind, I want you to remember that God lives in you and divinely guides your life each day. Therefore, there is no place where God cannot lead and guide you because He knows the plans for your future. There is nothing He cannot and will not reveal to you and nothing He cannot accomplish through you. All you need to do is to ask Him for His wisdom and guidance.

As you develop a deeper relationship with Jesus, He will direct your steps on the best path. He will never leave you nor abandon you. Jesus will keep the promises He has spoken into your heart. In the same way, you and I should honor our word because it can bring life to wounded souls.

Ruth did not abandon her words of commitment to Naomi, so Naomi returned home feeling a bit more secure. God, who is always involved in His children's affairs, noted Ruth's covenant words to Naomi and began orchestrating her steps toward her destiny.

Let me remind you God is listening to you and will bless you according to your words/declarations. Sometimes, we speak negatively about situations out of frustration instead of speaking life-giving words. When this occurs, remember to repent and recall the words quickly. Proverbs 18:21 says *death and life are in the power of the tongue, and those who love it and indulge it will eat its fruit and bear the consequences of their words.*

When you surrender to God and are willing to say yes to Him, He will divinely order your steps, and you will begin to experience His abundant favor. He will bless and grant you opportunities to help those in need. Many people have done amazing things because God helped, healed, rescued, and restored them. In return, they began to help others find hope and healing. I started this ministry seventeen years ago because of my hardships—health challenges, financial lack, family struggles, and disappointments. Despite being a hardworking employee and having job reviews that reflected my dedication, I had many seasons of unemployment. I must say I did not understand why.

The first couple of times I was unemployed, I complained a lot to God and sometimes against Him. I did not know why He would allow these things to happen in my life. I often reminded Him that I was a giver. Not only with my tithes and offerings, but I helped people, primarily single moms, with their children's needs.

I reasoned that since I was doing what He asked me to do, it was unreasonable for me to be in these hard seasons and unable to take care of my daily needs. What I missed during the first seasons of unemployment was this—God wanted to use this time to prepare me for my kingdom assignments. I could only see my struggles because I did not ask about His plans for my future. I could not pay my bills; therefore, this could not be His plan for me.

I found jobs that repeatedly ended with me being unemployed.

After the third unemployment season, I began to ask God what these seasons were designed to do. I discovered God wanted to use these times to deepen my prayer life and to do in-depth study of His Word. I was to spend each day praying and studying as though working an eight-hour shift.

With this new understanding, I began my days with hours of prayer and then hours studying His Word. I was being prepared but still needed to discover it was for a ministry assignment. An assignment entirely different from my background and work experience.

I grew in my relationship with God.

One day, I told Him that whenever He gave me a job, I would do all I could to help people in need. Unbeknownst to me, this was God's plan for my future. He had called me to teach His Word and help people in need worldwide. These difficult seasons were designed to prepare, train, and open my heart to His plans instead of my desires. The ministry journey has been challenging but beneficial. It has been worth all the challenges because of the many lives impacted worldwide.

Ruth had experienced hardships, and as a result, she had great compassion for Naomi. It was easier for Ruth to leave her homeland and help Naomi because her struggles birthed a desire to make a difference for the hurting. When you and I endure pain and suffering, we are more prone to be sympathetic and compassionate to others. Ruth felt Naomi's pain. She understood Naomi's suffering; therefore, helping Naomi was a natural reaction from one who also had a broken heart. God took notice and began directing Ruth's steps toward the divine destiny He had for her. Upon arriving in Bethlehem, Naomi's homeland, God ordered Ruth to the right place to find work. Ruth began to experience God's divine favor.

I defined the word 'divine' earlier. Now, let's look at the meaning of 'favor'. It means to have goodwill toward others. To esteem others highly. To show your approval. To be kind and to serve. *Luke 2:52 tells us that Jesus grew in wisdom and stature and in favor with God and man. 1 Samuel 2:26 says that the boy Samuel grew taller and grew in favor with the Lord and His people.*

Jesus and Samuel grew in favor first with God and then with people. You grow in favor with God when you please Him. How do you please Him? By obeying His will.

Notice, you must grow in favor with God before you will

gain favor with people. It is God who gives you favor with people. *Proverbs 8:35 says for whoever finds me finds life and receives favor from the Lord. Proverbs 3:3-4 says let love and faithfulness never leave you; bind them around your neck, write them on the tablet of your heart. Then you will win favor and a good name in the sight of God and man.*

The scriptures repeatedly state that you must FIRST find favor with God.

The Bible tells us when we find wisdom, we find favor with God. It is God who gives you favor with people. Ruth found favor with God, and God began aligning the right people with her, showering her with divine favor along the journey. She was loyal and kind in her interactions with Naomi, and the favor of God began to flow into her life.

Think about that for a moment. Loyalty and kindness are the doorways for how favor will begin to flow into your life.

***

Order My Steps

***

Now Naomi had a relative on her husband's side, from the clan of Elimelek, a man of standing, whose name was Boaz. And Ruth the Moabites said to Naomi, "Let me go to the fields and pick up the leftover grain behind anyone in whose eyes I find favor." Naomi said to her, "Go ahead, my daughter." So, she went out and began to glean in the fields behind the harvesters. As it turned out, she found herself working in a field belonging to Boaz, who was from the clan of Elimelek. Ruth 2:1-3 (NIV)

2 Thessalonians 3:10 says if a man does not work, he shall not eat. This verse is a clear message to remind us that work is a necessary part of life. Upon their arrival, Ruth understood that if Naomi and she were to survive, she had to find work. She asked Naomi for permission to look for work. God began to direct her steps and ordered them to Naomi's husband, Elimelek's family.

Throughout the Bible, you will find stories of how God always cared for the widows and the poor. He allowed the poor to glean in the fields of the wealthy. Gleaning gave people experiencing poverty the legal right to gather what was left by the reapers in the fields. The reapers were forbidden to reap to the very borders of their property. They could not go over the field again to gather the leftover crops. This food was God's provision for the poor. People experiencing poverty would go behind the reapers and pick up the remaining ears of corn and grapes. It was backbreaking work but necessary to sustain their lives. Naomi probably introduced Ruth to this Hebrew custom.

Ruth chapter two introduces us to Boaz, Naomi's family member. As we journey through this story, you will discover another family member who was a closer relative than Boaz. God did not mention him in the initial passage.

I see that God had already decided the path Ruth would take to her destiny. He had chosen Boaz as her husband over the other relative. As Ruth prepared to glean, she was divinely directed to Boaz's field.

Boaz was a man of 'standing' in the community. His position meant he was a man of valor—courage. Ruth was known as a woman of worth. Boaz's name means strength or to be strong.

In 1 Kings 7:21, we find something interesting. While

building the temple, King Solomon named the southern pillar Jakin—God will establish it, and the northern pillar Boaz—strength. It's evident Solomon depended on God and wanted to be surrounded by God's presence as he trusted God to complete the temple. God was His strength and would establish/finish what He started with Solomon.

Grab a hold of this: God is your strength, and He will establish/finish what He started in you. God directed Ruth to a man who could legally and financially care for her. God did not lead her to the field of the relative next in line before Boaz, even though this relative would be given the first opportunity to buy Elimelek's land and marry Ruth based on the laws of that century.

In Deuteronomy 25:5-6, a kinsman redeemer would purchase land belonging to the widow. He would marry her and have a child with her to continue the generational line. The kinsman redeemer was responsible for paying the debt and buying back property or possessions lost due to poverty. This role was to be undertaken by the relative who was next in line, but he refused to marry Ruth, so it was transferred to Boaz.

Why did God not choose this relative? Possibly, this relative was not God's first choice to be a part of the lineage of Jesus Christ. God knows people's hearts. He knew this relative would not submit to His plans for Ruth's future.

In choosing Boaz, God made a divine connection. He selected a man of character who would provide for Ruth and who was ordained to fulfill God's kingdom assignment on the earth. Boaz was the better choice, as you will see from the response of the other relative.

The divine connection God made with Ruth and Boaz was not just about their futures but also God's plan of redemption for humanity. Remember, God selects and works through people to accomplish His earthly plans.

As soon as she arrived at the field, Ruth began the back-breaking work of gleaning the field. She was not lazy or slothful as she began working in Boaz's field. When Boaz arrives, he sees Ruth, and we get a clear insight into his character.

He greeted his employees, declaring a blessing over them—respectful to those who worked for him. He asked, "Who does the young woman belong to?"

Notice he did not simply ask her name but who her family connection was. There was a level of respect in his question. He was checking to see who she belonged to and who was her covering and protection. In previous centuries and within some nationalities, the family, especially the fathers, were directly involved in choosing the spouses for their sons and daughters. Often, the children would remain living with their parents until they were married. This kept them under the protection and covering of the family name. Boaz was checking Ruth's family status.

Some may say that Ruth ended up in Boaz's field by coincidence, but NO, it was by God's sovereign will. God was working in her life as He is working in yours. God directs your steps to each assignment, relationship, job, etc., because He knows His plans for you based on Jeremiah 29:11. He plans to bless you and give you a hopeful future.

When you understand your assignments and the connections you make are divine, this will change the course of your destiny. You will look for God's presence anywhere and everywhere.

When you are experiencing delays, lack of resources, or long waiting seasons, determine that you will not be deterred. Ruth discovered there was nothing random in God's kingdom. God had planned and orchestrated her future. He has also planned your future and will direct your steps to your destiny. God wants His children to prosper in all areas of life. He set Ruth on a path to great prosperity because she said *yes* to Him.

Grace and Favor

So Boaz said to Ruth, "My daughter, listen to me. Don't go and glean in another field and don't go away from here. Stay here with the women who work for me. Watch the field where the men are harvesting, and follow along after the women. I have told the men not to lay a hand on you. And whenever you are thirsty, go and get a drink from the water jars the men have filled." At this, she bowed down with her face to the ground. She asked him, "Why have I found such favor in your eyes that you notice me —a foreigner?" Boaz replied, "I've been told all about what you have done for your mother-in-law since the death of your husband—how you left your father and mother and your homeland and came to live with a people you did not know before. May the Lord repay you for what you have done. May you be richly rewarded by the Lord, the God of Israel, under whose wings you have come to take refuge." "May I continue to find favor in your eyes, my lord," she said. "You have put me at ease by speaking kindly to your servant—though I do not have the standing of one of your servants." At mealtime Boaz said to her, "Come over here. Have some bread and dip it in the wine vinegar." When she sat down with the harvesters, he offered her some roasted grain. She ate all she wanted and had some left over. As she got up to glean, Boaz gave orders to his men, "Let her gather among the sheaves and don't reprimand her. Even pull out some stalks for her from the bundles and leave them for her to pick up, and don't rebuke her." So Ruth gleaned in the field until evening. Then she threshed the barley she had gathered, and it amounted to about an ephah.

    Ruth 2:8-17 (NIV)

Boaz had previously heard the story of Ruth's love and loyalty to Naomi. Remember, loyalty brings God's favor in your life. Therefore, Boaz felt kindly toward Ruth because she cared for Naomi, his relative. He approached Ruth and made her feel welcomed, safe, and protected. Boaz extended divine favor to her. He addressed her using the word, daughter. Historians say Boaz was approximately eighty, and Ruth was in her forties. She, indeed, could have been His daughter. He instructed Ruth to glean only in his fields while warning his workers to stay away from her, thus ensuring her safety. He took it a step further and provided water for her to drink, ensuring her physical comfort.

We see a beautiful portrait of grace as we look at Boaz's care and concern for Ruth. God, abundant in grace, provides for us in our needs. Grace gives us what we do not deserve. Grace provides favor in our lives. Grace protects us. Grace covers us. Grace gives us courage when facing difficulties because we find hope to make it through. Grace is one of the greatest gifts of God.

We should respond with heartfelt gratitude and thanks when grace is extended to us. Ruth showed deep gratitude to

Boaz. She fell on her face in humility, bowing down before him with a thankful heart. She did not yet understand the reason for this grace and favor she was being given, so she asked, *'Why'?*

Boaz's answer was simple. He had heard all that she had done for Naomi. She had left her father, mother, friends, homeland, and security and came to a foreign nation to keep watch over Naomi. Boaz was touched by her sacrifice and declared God's blessings over her.

Grab hold of these blessings for your life:

**May the Lord repay you for what you have done.
May you be richly rewarded by the Lord, the God of
Israel, under whose wings you have come to take refuge.**

As Boaz spoke these words, he declared God's blessings over Ruth. He first introduced her to His covenant-keeping God. Boaz prayed, asking God to be the protective presence around her because she had come to dwell under His wings. He introduced her to an aspect of God she had not yet discovered. She met Jehovah Jireh, our Provider.

The grace and favor shown to her lightened her heavy load. God's favor will lighten the burdens and loads you carry. It will sustain you when you feel like throwing in the towel because the journey is challenging.

Think about the many things you have done to aid those in

need. Now, listen and receive these words God is speaking over you.

He will bless you for all your efforts.
He will richly reward you for your sacrifice.
He will cover you and keep you safe.
He will be your refuge during every storm.
He SEES all you are doing and have done and will reward you accordingly.

We should respond as Ruth did when God pours
blessings into our lives.
She said, "May I continue to find favor in your eyes."

Not favor just in the moment but continually. This statement says Ruth expected to continue working in Boaz's fields and did not want to do anything to destroy this divine connection. She then expressed what was in her heart. "You have given me comfort and spoken kindly to your servant—though I don't have the standing of one of your servant girls." She recognized she had no status or position in her new role—she was less than his servants. Therefore, she was grateful for the extended mercy, grace, and favor she received. After this interaction, she resumed her backbreaking work, expecting nothing else from Boaz. She was grateful she had found a way to feed herself and Naomi.

God, however, was not finished pouring His blessings into her life.

At lunchtime, Boaz invited her to eat with him. She ate until she was full and had leftover food. As she returned to work, Boaz ordered his men not to embarrass her even if she gleaned among the sheaves. He recognized this was her first venture into this type of work. Favor abounded even more. He told his men to pull some stalks from their bundles and leave them for her to pick up and not to rebuke her. He gave her extra supplies.

I am always praying for an overflow of God's blessings in my life. How about you? Based on what Boaz did for Ruth, you and I can be assured that God will give us greater abundance. Notice Boaz started providing for her immediately, yet Ruth was unaware he was Naomi's relative. Ruth's heart was truly touched because she and Naomi had endured such hardships with all their losses. How extraordinary is God's compassion for us in our struggles? His compassion heals our souls.

Ruth received abundant provisions because she gave her life away for Naomi. God saw her sacrifice. Jesus is aware of your sacrifices. He rewards our faithfulness. Our hard work, labor of love, and devotion move Him.

Do you remember that Ruth had leftover food from her lunch with Boaz? She took it home not for herself but for Naomi, who was just as hungry as she had been. I want you to see this—in her need, she gave.

Ruth earned undeserved favor because she said *yes* to making a difference in someone else's life.

Steadfastness

So Ruth gleaned in the field until evening. Then she threshed the barley she had gathered, and it amounted to about an ephah. She carried it back to town, and her mother-in-law saw how much she had gathered. Ruth also brought out and gave her what she had left over after she had eaten enough. Her mother-in-law asked her, "Where did you glean today? Where did you work? Blessed be the man who took notice of you!" Then Ruth told her mother-in-law about the one at whose place she had been working. "The name of the man I worked with today is Boaz," she said. "The LORD bless him!" Naomi said to her daughter-in-law. "He has not stopped showing his kindness to the living and the dead." She added, "That man is our close relative; he is one of our guardian-redeemers." Then Ruth the Moabite said, "He even said to me, 'Stay with my workers until they finish harvesting all my grain.'" Naomi said to Ruth her daughter-in-law, "It will be good for you, my daughter, to go with the women who work for him, because in someone else's field you might be harmed." So Ruth stayed close to the women of Boaz to glean until the barley and wheat harvests were finished. And she lived with her mother-in-law. Ruth 2:17-23 (NIV)

Some of us have had hardships and painful seasons in our lives. We have had to decide how to move forward when facing them. Will we give up when the way seems complicated, or will we press through until our deliverance comes? Ruth was in a hard season, but she remained steadfast.

She gleaned in the field from morning until evening—constantly bending over to retrieve the leftover barley. When she was done gleaning, she had to beat the stalks to get to the grains. She gleaned over a bushel of grain in one day's harvest, weighing approximately sixty pounds. Her work was not complete. She still had to carry it home on her shoulders.

Pause briefly and consider how you would have handled this load even if you only had to take it a short distance.

All through these hardships, she remained steadfast. She did not complain. *Help us, Jesus.* She did not curse the faith that brought her into this painful season in her life. She did not give up. She did not blame God or lose faith during her assignment. She maintained an attitude of thanksgiving for God's provision.

Let me ask the questions. Are you challenged by what you just read? Do you remain thankful in the hard seasons? Do you complain against God? ***Ouch!*** I have done all of the above at various times.

Could we have delayed our breakthroughs because of our negative attitudes during difficult seasons? The scriptures bear this out. Let's take a moment and look at Moses and the Israelites' struggles.

Now the people complained about their hardships in the hearing of the LORD, and when he heard them his anger was aroused. Then fire from the LORD burned among them and consumed some of the outskirts of the camp. When the people cried out to Moses, he prayed to the LORD and the fire died down. So that place was called Taberah, because fire from the LORD had burned among them. The rabble with them began to crave other food, and again the Israelites started wailing and said, "If only we had meat to eat! We remember the fish we ate in Egypt at no cost—also the cucumbers, melons, leeks, onions and garlic. But now we have lost our appetite; we never see anything but this manna!" The manna was like coriander seed and looked like resin. The people went around gathering it, and then ground it in a hand mill or crushed it in a mortar. They cooked it in a pot or made it into loaves. And it tasted like something made with olive oil. When the dew settled on the camp at night, the manna also came down. Moses heard the people of every family wailing at the entrance to their tents. The LORD became exceedingly angry, and Moses was troubled. He asked the LORD, "Why have you brought this trouble on your servant? What have I done to displease you that you put the burden of all these people on me? Did I conceive all these people? Did I give them birth? Why do you tell me to carry them in my arms, as a nurse carries an infant, to the land you promised on oath to their ancestors? Where can I get meat for all these people? They keep wailing to me, 'Give us meat to eat!' I cannot carry all these people by myself; the

burden is too heavy for me. If this is how you are going to treat
me, please go ahead and kill me—if I have found favor in your
eyes—and do not let me face my own ruin."
   Numbers 11:1-15 (NIV)

───────────

Because the people he led were complaining about him,
Moses began to complain to God and question Him. Did you
catch it? Every single one of the Israelites complained about
Moses and Aaron. We are talking about multiple thousands of
people who wished the Lord had killed them in Egypt.

They reminisced about all the food they ate while living in
Egyptian bondage. They complained about the food God
provided on their journey, forgetting the oppression they were
under by those Egyptian taskmasters. Did they forget that God
had freed them from slavery as they complained about their
wants? Notice they were not hungry. Their *needs* were unmet,
but their *wants* were met.

God said He would rain down manna from heaven. Then,
He tested the people. They were only to gather enough food for
one day's meal, and on the sixth day, they were commanded to
gather two days' meal, so they would not work on the Sabbath,
their day of rest from laboring. God wanted to see their obedience level if they would follow His command—only gathering
enough food for one day. Some still did not obey Him.

Following God's lead, Moses told them God would give
them meat in the evening and bread in the morning so they
would know God was God. He reminded them they were
complaining against God and that He heard all their grumbling.
They were to gather only the amount they needed. Some gath-

ered a little, while others gathered a lot. When they measured it, they all received the exact amounts they needed. What a lesson for them and us. God knew what they needed. God promised to take care of our needs, *not* our wants. This statement bears repeating. Many times, we grumble about our wants and not about our needs. God keeps His promises and meets our needs just as He said He would.

Some Israelites went out on the Sabbath looking for manna but found none. They disobeyed God.

Often, when we complain, it is not because God has not met our needs; it's our wants we are complaining about. God did not tell us He would take care of our wants. He tells us He will take care of our needs according to His riches in glory by Christ Jesus (Philippians 4:19). The Israelites complained that Moses brought them into the wilderness to starve them to death.

Did they forget that the One who had delivered them was listening? Their complaint was not just about Moses and Aaron but also about God, their Deliverer.

In Numbers 11, we see even after all God provided, the Israelites were still dissatisfied and continued to complain. This time, when God heard them, He did something about it. He sent fire and incinerated the outer skirts of the camp. This display scared the Israelites. Moses had to pray for them, and God caused the fire to die down.

They then craved other food and began wailing. They wanted fish, cucumbers, melons, leeks, onions and garlic. They were essentially telling God they never get anything from Him but manna. Manna was the Bread of God, and they were rejecting it. The Bible said God was furious, and Moses was troubled.

Moses was fed up and asked God why He had brought this

trouble on him, His servant. He then began to complain to God about the responsibility He was assigned. The people's attitudes and actions affected Moses and caused him to do something He had never done before—complain to God.

Moses said:

"What have I done to displease you that you put the burden of all these people on me? Did I give them birth? Why do you tell me to carry them in my arms, as a nurse carries an infant, to the land you promised on oath to their ancestors? Where can I get meat for all these people? They keep wailing to me. I cannot carry all these people by myself; the burden is too heavy for me. If this is how you are going to treat me, please go ahead and kill me—if I have found favor in your eyes—and do not let me face my ruin."

The complaining Israelites caused Moses to go to God with His complaints. He told God to kill him if the situation was not going to change. Their complaining caused him to do something out of the norm—challenge God. He was overloaded. He began to regret the responsibilities he was assigned. The people pushed him to the breaking point. It is crucial to note that instead of lashing out at the people, he cried out to the only One who could change the situation.

People can cause us to do things we would not otherwise do. Moses was not a complainer. He trusted God. Yet, the people's attitude caused him to murmur and complain to the One who had done so many incredible things through him. Let me encourage you not to allow the negativity you hear to change your position of trusting God, no matter your hardships. Ruth did not murmur or complain about her struggles. She did not blame God. Let's return to her story.

When Ruth arrived home to Naomi, not only did she bring the grains she had gleaned, but she was able to feed Naomi with her leftover lunch. Ruth was thoughtful, kind, and generous in her struggles. She did not think only about her needs. Thinking of others when struggling is challenging because we want to focus on ourselves during trouble. I am painting this picture because many of us can attest that some people can be selfish and unwilling to help others who are struggling. They want to hold on to the little they have, hoping it will last.

Jesus tells us in Luke 6:38 to *'Give, and it will be given to us. A good measure, pressed down, shaken together and running over, will be poured into your lap."* Have you ever wondered why the scripture did not stop at *give, and it shall be given to you*? We can easily understand that message. Jesus wants us to have abundance.

What is a good measure? In Hebrew, it means to stretch out, to extend, and to spread out. It's a specified amount. Jesus says even though you may pay for *a single measure*, you will receive much more than you paid for because God will add more to you. As He adds more, you will be blessed and can generously give to others in need.

What is the meaning of *press down and shaken together*? When we press something down and shake it, it settles, and we can add more to the container. This example is the abundance that Jesus desires to pour into our lives. His measure, a specified amount, is so considerable we cannot hold it in our hands since they are not large enough to contain His immeasurable supply. His blessings will overflow into our lives. This is why the scripture says His measure is poured into our laps. The scripture not only talks about financial blessings but also refers to the blessings of the Spirit. Jesus wants you to be abundantly blessed in your health, finances, emotions, and every aspect of life. He died to ensure these blessings.

God opened a door for Ruth to experience this type of blessing. Naomi was amazed by all the barley Ruth brought home and asked where she had worked. Upon learning it was in Boaz's field, she instantly knew this was a divine connection from God. Naomi had wanted to be bitter against God, but God was demonstrating His love and care for each of them. He had not forgotten her and showed this through His immediate provisions. His favor and kindness were abounding in their lives. Before telling Ruth who Boaz was, Naomi gave thanks to God.

———

She did what was most important—showed
sincere appreciation for the blessings.

———

Ruth gleaned only in Boaz's field for the rest of the season, and God provided abundantly. She was steadfast in her devotion to Naomi, never murmuring or complaining about her backbreaking work or the low social position. She handled these menial tasks with great courage, grace, and humility. God took notice.

Ruth understood something many of us know: working is necessary for survival. Therefore, she applied herself to each task with great determination. God's plan of redemption was unfolding around her even though she was unaware of it. Some of us have prevented God's plans from working seamlessly because we won't cooperate with Him. When things get complicated, we balk and either quit or develop an attitude and refuse to be diligent. These attitudes will not get you the results you desire. They will delay you getting to your promised land. Do you want the best God has for you? Then, you must be willing to do it His way. There is no way to more tremendous success but through Him. He is the doorway you and I must enter to receive His promises for our lives. Let me highlight a few scriptures that give us the meaning of favor:

- *Proverbs 11:27 – If you search for good, you will find favor.*
- *Proverbs 16:15 – when the king smiles, there is life; his favor refreshes like a spring rain. (Is the King smiling at you?).*
- *Proverbs 22:1 – a good name is rather to be chosen than great riches, loving favor rather than silver and gold.*
- *Psalm 84:11 – For the Lord is our sun and shield. He gives us grace and glory. The Lord will withhold no good thing from those who do what is right.*
- *Acts 7:46 – David found favor with God and asked for the privilege of building a permanent temple for the God of Jacob. (What will you do for God as He favors you?)*

You must learn to walk, live, and abide (remain, dwell, continue, and stay) in God's favor because it will enrich your life in many ways. Do you want to know how to experience God's favor?

Here are some clues:

- Be committed to Him.
- Follow through on your word.
- Seek after godly wisdom.
- Be loyal.
- Be kind.
- Be a hard worker.
- Look for God in all the circumstances of life.
- Be thankful.
- Be humble.
- Be unselfish.

Don't give up because God's favor will find you.

As you examine your life in light of the lessons in this chapter, I pray you see what you need to do to experience God's divine favor and His great abundance each day of your life. *Psalm 84:11(b) reminds us that God does not withhold anything good from those whose walk is blameless, those who do what is right.* Ruth did what was right, and she was rewarded.

You will be rewarded for doing the right things. Remember, God is watching your walk and also your talk. Keep pressing forward and become unstoppable.

CHAPTER 5
Is It Godly Wisdom?

Sometimes, we feel we are operating in Godly wisdom only to discover it is natural. We think others are giving us wise counsel and godly wisdom, but despite appearance, that is only sometimes what we receive. Do you know there are two types of wisdom? Yes, Godly wisdom (heavenly wisdom) and earthly wisdom (man's wisdom). Let me explore this with you.

Godly wisdom is when God speaks to you and gives you direction about your life—a job, promotion, your life partner, etc. When you follow His instructions, you reap the right results and receive the benefits. Wise counsel is when someone gives you a word that helps you make better decisions. Many years ago, before I knew God called me to ministry, I was at an event, and a gentleman said, "God is going to use you powerfully around the world; remember to clothe yourself with humility." I received this wise counsel/words and have worked diligently to make this a part of my daily life. Natural wisdom is when you assess a situation and decide based on what you think is best. An example of natural wisdom is choosing to move to another state without prior planning or having the means to support yourself upon arrival.

Wisdom is vital to our lives, and we find rich wisdom nuggets throughout the Bible, especially in the book of Proverbs. God desires to infuse wisdom into the lives of children.

- Wisdom combats the enemy's attacks.
- It helps us to make right, godly decisions.
- It helps us to succeed by aiding us as we seek to live rich, full lives.
- We need wisdom for daily living.

Luke 2:52 tells us Jesus grew in wisdom and stature and in favor with God and man. I previously shared this scripture that Jesus grew in favor with God. I want to look at another part of the verse as it relates directly to you. Each day, my staff and I declare this scripture over our lives and insert our names behind Jesus. Why? We strive to be like Him and to accomplish His plans on earth. So, adopting His words for our lives will help us to achieve His plans. I invite you to make this scripture a part of your daily life so you, too, can receive all the wisdom, blessings, and favor God wants you to have.

As I already mentioned, there are two types of wisdom. Heavenly wisdom and earthly wisdom. James 3:17 tells us that heavenly wisdom comes from God. It is pure. It is faithful to God's will. It is peaceable, gentle, and full of mercy. It produces good fruit and produces fruits of righteousness.

In James 3:13-16, earthly wisdom is defined as wisdom that confuses. It produces evil fruits. It's temporal and worldly. This type of wisdom does not lead to a successful life since it is based on our fleshly desires that can lead us to be envious, jealous, or selfish in our actions and attitudes. It's sensual, which means it appeals to our senses and emotions. It is demonic and influenced by the devil. Many people operate in earthly wisdom more often than heavenly wisdom. You and I must consistently pursue Jesus to be guided in every season to achieve the right results based on our decisions.

Godly wisdom will help us to avert disasters in our lives.

With that focus, let's take a deep dive into the wisdom and guidance Naomi gave Ruth to determine if this was godly wisdom, natural wisdom, or wise counsel. After discovering Boaz was the one who took care of Ruth's needs, Naomi began to plan.

At the conclusion of Ruth chapter two, Naomi declared a blessing from the Lord over Boaz for his excellent care of Ruth. She spoke of his kindness to the living and the dead, meaning her, her husband, and their children. She told Ruth Boaz was a close relative and one of their kinsman-redeemers. One of God's covenant promises is His loving kindness to His people. Naomi and Ruth were experiencing this.

During that century, a kinsman-redeemer was a close relative who had influence. Members of the extended family would go to this person for help, especially when their possessions were in danger of being lost to them. He was responsible for buying back the family land during crises. He also had the responsibility of buying back his relatives who were in slavery (Leviticus 25:47-49). In Deuteronomy 25:5-10, another primary duty was to provide heirs for his deceased brother. The kinsman-redeemer also avenged the killing of relatives and provided care, concern, and help during difficult seasons.

God provided this support to the Israelites. He was their Redeemer. He was their closest family member who regularly stepped in and restored them when they were in dire situations. In the upcoming chapters, I will share more about Jesus, our Messiah, our Kinsman-Redeemer. Remember, in Ruth 2:8, which we read earlier, Boaz encouraged Ruth to stay with his female workers to safeguard her from harm. Naomi encouraged her to do the same. Ruth complied and continued to glean in Boaz's fields until the barley and wheat harvest seasons were completed.

These harvests lasted until March or April.

Ruth and Naomi had arrived home in early March, the beginning of these harvests. Sometime during this short time-frame, Naomi devised her plan to marry Ruth to Boaz. Naomi was operating in earthly wisdom. Ruth had only known Boaz briefly when Naomi went to work to secure her future.

———

One day Ruth's mother-in-law Naomi said to her, "My daughter, I must find a home for you, where you will be well provided for. Now Boaz, with whose women you have worked, is a relative of ours. Tonight, he will be winnowing barley on the threshing floor. Wash, put on perfume, and get dressed in your best clothes. Then go down to the threshing floor, but don't let him know you are there until he has finished eating and drinking. When he lies down, note the place where he is lying. Then go and uncover his feet and lie down. He will tell you what to do." "I will do whatever you say," Ruth answered. So, she went down to the threshing floor and did everything her mother-in-law told her to do.

Ruth 3:1-6 (NIV)

Naomi began to plan Ruth's future because she recognized God had orchestrated Ruth's steps to Boaz's field. She did not tell Ruth she was trying to find a husband but a home for her. What is the difference? A home means a place of safety, peace, and the end of uncertainties. Naomi attempted to permanently settle Ruth within a family that would love, support, and care for her. Ruth would find fulfillment and financial security within this home. In the above scripture, Naomi told her to bathe and perfume herself and gave her specific instructions on how to win over Boaz.

Let me ask the question: Were these instructions godly wisdom or earthly wisdom? Let's search the scriptures together to answer these questions. Naomi's instructions to Ruth to bathe, dress, and perfume herself sound like she was planning a seduction, right? It sounds like several stories in the Old Testament that reflected sexual overtones. That was not Naomi's true intention, but these scriptures question her recommendation. Let's look at a few of those to determine if her instructions were wise.

Noah, man of soil, proceeded to plant a vineyard. When he drank some of its wine, he became drunk and lay uncovered inside his tent. Ham, the father of Canaan, saw his father's nakedness and told his two brothers outside.
Genesis 9:20-22 (NIV)

One day the older daughter said to the younger, "Our father is old, and there's no man around here to lie with us, as is the custom all over the earth. Let's get our father to drink wine and then lie with him and preserve our family line through our father." That night, they got their father to drink wine, and the older daughter went in and lay with him. He was not aware of it when she lay down or when she got up. The next day the older daughter said to the younger, "Last night I lay with my father. Let's get him to drink wine again tonight, and you go in and lie with him so we can preserve our family line through our father.
Genesis 19:31-34 (NIV)

Later, I passed by, and when I looked at you and saw that you were old enough for love, I spread the corner of my garment over you and covered your nakedness. I gave you my solemn oath and entered into a covenant with you, declares the Sovereign Lord, and you became mine.
Ezekiel 16:8-9 (NIV)

So, the next day the people rose early and sacrificed burnt offerings and presented fellowship offerings. Afterward, they sat down to eat and drink and got up to indulge in revelry. Then the Lord said to Moses, "Go down, because your people, whom you brought up out of Egypt, have become corrupt.
Exodus 32:6-7 (NIV)

When David was told, "Uriah did not go home," he asked
him, "Haven't you just come from a distance? Why didn't you go
home?" Uriah said to David, "The ark and Israel and Judah are
staying in tents, and my master Joab and my lord's men are
camped in the open fields. How could I go to my house to eat and
drink and lie with my wife? As surely as you live, I will not do
such a thing!"
   2 Samuel 11:10 (NIV)

———

Ruth was a Moabite. Earlier, I told you she was from the
lineage of Lot, whose daughters had an incestuous relationship
with their father to produce children and persevere the lineage.
As you study the Bible, the Moabites' women seduced the
Israeli men at Baal Poer (Numbers 25:2). Therefore, a marriage
to a Moabite was considered sinful for Israeli men
(Deuteronomy 23:3). Naomi's instructions to this Moabite
woman, Ruth, could be misconstrued. They look fishy. People
could assume that she was trying to get Ruth to seduce Boaz.
For Ruth to go to the harvest under the cover of night does not
seem like godly wisdom.

Naomi knew the men would drink after a good harvest
season; therefore, some would be drunk. Her directives to Ruth
seemed unsound and needed more heavenly wisdom. Something untoward could have happened, but God was a step
ahead of her plans. As an obedient daughter, Ruth listened and
obeyed Naomi's instructions.

Ruth did not follow the instructions to the letter. She
injected her own wisdom which ended up paying dividends.

She did not follow the instructions to the letter. She did not try to seduce him, which was implied in Naomi's instructions. Ruth uncovered Boaz's feet and laid down. She did not awaken him. When he awakened and discovered someone lying there, he was startled and asked who it was.

Go back to the verse and look at Ruth's answer. You will again see a level of great wisdom in Ruth's response. Before this event, she was referred to as Ruth the Moabites. She does not give that title to Boaz. She changes her status to Ruth, your maid.

Think about that for a moment. What does a maid do? She is a helper. She serves the people for whom she works. She is a household servant who washes, cooks, and cleans. A maid in biblical times was an unmarried girl. Ruth identifies herself to Boaz as one who serves and gives help to her master.

Again, Ruth deviated from Naomi's instructions. She did not wait for Boaz to tell her what to do; she told him what she desired. Ruth asked him to fulfill his biblical covenant by marrying her. She did not ask about a home, as Naomi had stated, but instead, she asked him to marry her. She got right to the point and said what her needs were.

The story of Tamar in Genesis 35 tells us why Ruth could make this request. Even though the passage is long, it has several vital truths—having integrity, keeping your pledge, and honoring your word. This story is intriguing and worth reading.

About this time, Judah left home and moved to Adullam, where he stayed with a man named Hirah. There he saw a

Canaanite woman, the daughter of Shua, and he married her. When he slept with her, she became pregnant and gave birth to a son, and he named the boy Er. Then she became pregnant again and gave birth to another son, and she named him Onan. And when she gave birth to a third son, she named him Shelah. At the time of Shelah's birth, they were living at Kezib. In the course of time, Judah arranged for his firstborn son, Er, to marry a young woman named Tamar. But Er was a wicked man in the Lord's sight, so the Lord took his life. Then Judah said to Er's brother Onan, "Go and marry Tamar, as our law requires of the brother of a man who has died. You must produce an heir for your brother." But Onan was not willing to have a child who would not be his own heir. So, whenever he had intercourse with his brother's wife, he spilled the semen on the ground. This prevented her from having a child who would belong to his brother. But the Lord considered it evil for Onan to deny a child to his dead brother. So, the Lord took Onan's life, too. Then Judah said to Tamar, his daughter-in-law, "Go back to your parents' home and remain a widow until my son Shelah is old enough to marry you." (But Judah didn't really intend to do this because he was afraid Shelah would also die, like his two brothers.) So, Tamar went back to live in her father's home. Some years later, Judah's wife died. After the time of mourning was over, Judah and his friend Hirah the Adullamite went up to Timnah to supervise the shearing of his sheep. Someone told Tamar, "Look, your father-in-law is going up to Timnah to shear his sheep." Tamar was aware that Shelah had grown up, but no arrangements had been made for her to come and marry him. So, she changed out of her widow's clothing and covered herself with a veil to disguise herself. Then she sat beside the road at the entrance to the village of Enaim, which is on the road to Timnah. Judah noticed her and thought she was a prostitute, since she had covered her face. So, he stopped and proposi-

tioned her. "Let me have sex with you," he said, not realizing that she was his own daughter-in-law. "How much will you pay to have sex with me?" Tamar asked. "I'll send you a young goat from my flock," Judah promised. "But what will you give me to guarantee that you will send the goat?" she asked. "What kind of guarantee do you want?" he replied. She answered, "Leave me your identification seal and its cord and the walking stick you are carrying." So, Judah gave them to her. Then he had intercourse with her, and she became pregnant. Afterward, she went back home, took off her veil, and put on her widow's clothing as usual.

　　Genesis 38:1-19 (NLT)

　　This type of marriage was known as the levirate marriage—marriage to a brother-in-law. This story shows why Ruth could appeal to Boaz to marry her. This was one of the rights given by God to the widows to ensure their lineage would endure. Being married protected the widows. Additionally, a widowed woman's eldest son would care for her financial needs to ensure she did not end up in poverty. Deuteronomy 25:5 tells us God's purpose for this type of marriage. It was to carry on the name of the dead brother so that their name would not be blotted out from Israel. Since both of Naomi's sons were dead, the relative who was next in line would take on these responsibilities. Boaz accepted the responsibility of taking care of Ruth's needs.

　　This story could have been written in our modern-day time. It is so sensational. I have chosen to highlight this story because it shows us God expects us to have integrity when dealing with one another. Ruth expected Boaz to abide by these standards just as God expected Judah and his sons to honor their promises to Tamar.

Let me summarize the story for you. Tamar's plan to sleep with her father-in-law was a result of him not honoring his word to her. He chose not to give her his third son, Selah, fearing his death. Judah, her father-in-law, thought Tamar was responsible for the deaths of his two sons. She was not. God destroyed them because of their wickedness in not following His directives in dealing with the widow, Tamar.

When Judah heard that Tamar, his daughter-in-law, was pregnant, he demanded that she be brought to him and for her to be burned to death because she had committed prostitution. As they prepared to burn to death, she sent this message to her father-in-law: "The man who owns these things made me pregnant. Look closely. Whose seal and cord and walking stick are these?" Judah recognized them immediately and said, "She is more righteous than I am because I didn't arrange for her to marry my son, Shelah." Yes, Tamar had acted more righteously and godly than Judah.

Ruth's story was similar to Tamar's in that each sought to extend their generations, giving them a place and rights within the Israeli lineage.

Let me ask: Do you keep your word? Listen, God hears every word we speak and expects us to keep our promises, especially when it is one of His Covenant promises. Even while giving his word, Judah had no intention of sharing Selah with Tamar. He was attempting to keep him alive since he believed she was the reason for his other sons' deaths. How interesting that he would think she was responsible for their deaths instead of acknowledging that their wickedness against God caused their deaths. Yet, God still expected Judah to keep His covenant and honor his word to Tamar. God truly takes our covenant promises seriously.

This story and many others throughout the Bible show that a male relative would produce children by their brother's widows to keep the family line intact. So, Ruth, in speaking to Boaz, asked him to keep this same covenant promise to her so Elimelek and Naomi's lineage would continue.

Boaz told her about a relative who was ahead of him in purchasing Naomi's husband's property. This closer relative had to be allowed to fulfill this obligation before Boaz could marry Ruth and acquire the property.

Do you think Naomi was unaware of this relative? She may have felt Boaz was a better match for Ruth. We will look further at this story in the upcoming chapter.

Boaz recognized what Naomi had done in setting this stage for Ruth which had negative implications, so he protected her. Boaz did not follow through on what Naomi implied when she sent Ruth to his side in the dead of night. He responded to Ruth's request to fulfill his covenant obligation. This unwise recommendation of Naomi's, which could have been disastrous, was averted. God was glorified in Ruth's and Boaz's actions because they demonstrated wisdom and integrity in their dealings with each other.

In contrasting earthly wisdom, which is sensual, to heavenly wisdom, which is pure, we must remember some things. Many people today are often evil, just as it has been recorded in many verses in the Bible. Following these people's lead is often tricky without consulting God for proper directions.

Remember, Ruth was a new believer. She still needed to understand this new journey's rules and regulations thoroughly. Ruth did not yet know the character or nature of the Israelites' God or how He operated. She also needed to discern what acceptable practices were for the Jewish people and which were not. Since Naomi was her teacher, naturally, she followed her lead. As a Moabite woman whose ancestors made many immoral decisions, she knew that the recommendations, if followed thoroughly, would lead her down the wrong path, so she aborted them. Let's recall that the Moabite's lineage was filled with atrocities and immoral relationships, so Ruth chose a higher moral standard in declaring she was a servant. She faced and overcame a moral and character test. Unbeknownst to her, God was already at work directing her steps and realigning her actions to produce the right results for her future.

Think about times when you used your natural earthly wisdom, which led to a bad outcome or disaster. Some of you may have genuinely felt that you were making the best choices but did not consult God. I am thinking of my many wrong decisions over the years and thankful for God's intervention.

One of those decisions was to buy a car that was a stick shift, even though I did not know how to drive a vehicle with a manual transmission. The first day driving to work on a busy roadway was stressful and embarrassing. After stalling many times, a gentleman came over to ask if I needed help, only to discover nothing was wrong with my car; I hadn't learned how to drive a stick shift vehicle. With a disgusted look, he walked away. I am still mortified as I write this example. There, indeed, was no wisdom in that decision. By God's grace, I eventually learned how to drive the car. However, when it was time to replace it, I purchased a vehicle with an automatic transmission.

When we think of heavenly wisdom, we discover only God can lead and direct our steps and lives. So, with that in mind, we must consult Him for all decisions, tiny or significant. His directives make for an easier, more peaceful existence.

Wisdom will give you the best results in life. One of my favorite passages in the Bible is Proverbs 3. As I share some life-enriching nuggets from this passage, I invite you to make wisdom a daily part of your life. Ask God to fill you with His wisdom each day so you can make decisions that align with His will for you and fill your life with His abundant blessings.

Proverbs 3:1-26 – Wisdom Tips:

- *The first notable thing is that God calls wisdom, 'she.'*
- Wisdom brings well-being.
- It prolongs your life.
- It brings you peace.
- It brings you prosperity.
- You will gain favor and a good name with wisdom.
- It brings health to your body and nourishes your bones.
- You are blessed when you find wisdom.
- She is more profitable to you than silver.
- She yields better returns than gold.
- She is more precious than rubies.
- Nothing you desire can compare to her.
- In her right hand is life.
- In her left hand are riches and honor.

- Her ways are pleasant.
- Her paths are filled with peace.
- She is a tree of life to those who take hold of her.
- Those who hold her fast will be blessed.
- The earth's foundation was laid by wisdom.
- Wisdom will grace your neck.
- Wisdom will keep you safe.
- When you lie down, your sleep will be sweet.
- There is no need to fear sudden disaster since wisdom is guarding you.
- The Lord is at your side and will keep you from falling into the traps of the enemy.

Ruth operated in godly wisdom in all her decisions. She obeyed Boaz and only worked in his fields with the other women. She was attentive to Naomi and was respectful in her dealings, even when she might not have understood or agreed with recommendations or instructions. She waited patiently for Boaz to resolve the issues with the other relative to ensure their marriage would take place. Using Godly wisdom ensured Ruth's safety, blessings, and favor with God and others. All these promises are yours when *wisdom* is the cornerstone of your life.

———

I conclude this chapter with a challenge for you.
GET WISDOM AT ANY COST.
Wisdom will protect you. Love her, and she will watch over you. Cherish her, and she will exalt you.

———

Ruth operated in wisdom and experienced all these things; you can, too. Wisdom will cause you to be unstoppable.

CHAPTER 6
Redeemed

J esus is our Kinsman-Redeemer. Boaz was only a dim
reflection of Him. The blood Jesus shed at Calvary has
redeemed you and me. Without the shedding of His
blood, we would not experience absolute freedom. God
sent Jesus to ransom, rescue, recover, and liberate humanity.
Jesus' shed blood bought our freedom and reconnected us to
the right relationship with our Father, God.

Jesus' earthly assignment was to reconcile us to God, who
created us to be members of His family. By dying on the cross at
Calvary, Jesus fulfilled His assignment. From the time God
created Adam and Eve until today, it was all about having a
family.

God wanted intimate fellowship with a people who had
their own will. The angels and the heavenly hosts must do what
God commands. They are subjected to God's will. In creating
humankind, God gave us the ability to choose. We can say *yes* or
no to Him. When He breathed life into Adam and Eve, He also
allowed them to determine right from wrong. They could

choose Him out of love and over their desires. From the story in Genesis, we know that they chose their desires over Him.

God did not force Adam or Eve to love Him enough to choose Him. Likewise, God does not force us to obey Him because He says so. We choose to obey Him out of love. God has also given us the right to choose our path. He gave Adam and Eve life in the garden but allowed them to make their own choices. Because God gave her free will, Eve chose the path of disobedience. Her choices and Adam's collaboration led to the need for redemption to restore our relationship with God.

Jesus is our redemption.

Have you considered your need for redemption? Jesus desires you to live in freedom. He shed His blood on your behalf to ransom you and restore you to the right relationship with God. He gave His life in exchange for yours because you are special to Him. He wants an intimate relationship with you.

God directed Ruth's steps to her divine destiny in the previous chapter. He took what she had, her love and commitment to Naomi, and used it to pour His abundant blessings into her life. God lifted Ruth from a pagan nation and utilized her because He knew her heart was right for the assignment. She enriched Naomi's life.

Ruth not only helped Naomi deal with the pain in her life but also helped her carry her burdens. Titus 2:4 tells us that older women must train the younger ones to manage their homes and families. While Ruth was assisting Naomi, Naomi was preparing Ruth for her future.

Consider the generation in which we currently live. Do you see many older women training and equipping the young ones? Those being trained live and act differently from everyone else. If older men and women were preparing the next generation, we would see more significant growth in the younger generation's lives. Our lives would be more enriched by the sharing of wisdom that comes with age. We could possibly see less chaos in the world.

While they were in Moab, Naomi had urged Ruth to return to her homeland and family to ensure she would remarry and have a family. Since Ruth chose to stay with Naomi, she made it her job to secure a home and family for Ruth. Naomi sought to eliminate and address Ruth's financial and familial challenges. She wanted Ruth to have personal fulfillment, and during that century, this came from marriage and raising a family.

Do you know anyone, especially a woman, who does not desire to be secure in life? Isn't the desire of many people to feel loved and accepted into a family unit? As I previously shared in the chapter, God designed us to be His family. Our great King also desires to experience closeness with humankind. Therefore, it is not surprising we have the same desire to be a part of a family unit.

Ruth returned and reported what happened during the night's meeting with Boaz. Naomi gave Ruth another piece of advice. In Ruth 3:18, She said, *"Just be patient my daughter, until we hear what happens. The man won't rest until he has settled things today."* Be patient. How many of you are challenged just hearing the word patience? I am, too.

———

I have struggled with being patient for a very long time. Why is it so hard for us to wait for things to manifest? We all desire immediate results in the things we hope and pray for. Very often, these things manifest outside our time frame. Usually, we expect to get immediate answers and breakthroughs, but it does not always happen at the moment we pray. I say this often: we know many things about God but do not understand His perfect time for us. Therefore, we have to wait. Waiting is hard. It does not mean God will not answer you; you must wait for Him to move on your behalf. He will manifest His Word and promises in your life.

———

I love the Word of God, but many years ago, I discovered this scripture, 2 Peter 3:8, and if I am honest, it is not one I go to often. I know I must embrace and apply the Word of God to all areas of my life, even when challenged by it.

Listen to the scripture, *"But don't forget this one thing dear friends: With the Lord one day is like a thousand years, and a thousand years are like one day."*

I am still challenged even as I type it. It says I must be patient. I must wait. I must keep hoping. I must keep believing. These statements speak loudly and clearly—be patient and wait for the appointed time. I am still waiting for many things to unfold in my life. After so many years of being patient, it is still hard to wait. Sometimes, the situations and plans become more apparent when I wait for God, but it is still hard.

One day, I went to the bank. I entered the shortest drive-through line, and the people ahead of me took excessive time to complete their transactions. After sitting through two additional transactions, I decided not to wait any longer and moved to a line moving more swiftly despite having more vehicles.

When I pulled up to the kiosk and reached for the canister, to my dismay, it was not there. I buzzed the teller and was told the person just before me had driven off with it. My disappointment and irritation were palpable. Can you guess which was now the shortest line? Yep, the line I had vacated. I am laughing at myself as I type this.

As I sat waiting to make my deposit, I felt as if the Lord was laughing and enjoying what was turning into a teaching moment for me. He began talking to me about my patience, as He has done many times before. I was reminded of the many times I have moved from line to line in grocery stores and other places throughout my journey of learning patience. Some of you can tell your own story of learning patience.

Naomi asked Ruth to be patient and wait to hear what happens. Patience is the key. As we wait patiently, God is working. Our problem is that we cannot see His work, so we don't know how far He is in the process. Naomi expected God to move and for there to be a good outcome. She did not know if Boaz would move slowly or quickly, but her dependence was not on Boaz but God, who was already at work in their situation.

Naomi could see from a spiritual perspective that God was already at work orchestrating the events of Ruth's future. She was at peace with the waiting. I need to find peace as I wait. How about you? This peace comes from knowing and trusting God to give us His best for our lives. Naomi added one last thing that reassured Ruth: the man will not rest until he has settled things today. She expected the answer to arrive swiftly. Naomi knew she would not have to wait long. We don't often have this insight and reassurance in our waiting seasons. Some results are only sometimes immediate. I'm currently in one of those waiting seasons. This one is among my most challenging because it is attached to my kingdom assignments. We must all rest, wait, hope, and trust in God's faithfulness. I am learning to be more patient. How about you?

The Kinsman Redeemer

After speaking with Ruth, Boaz immediately talked to the next-in-line relative to secure Naomi's late husband's property. He did not delay. Boaz did not try to find another solution to the problem. He took action and did what he had committed to do.

Meanwhile, Boaz went up to the town gate and sat down there just as the guardian-redeemer he had mentioned came along. Boaz said, "Come over here, my friend, and sit down." So he went over and sat down. Boaz took ten of the elders of the town and said, "Sit here," and they did so. Then he said to the guardian-redeemer, "Naomi, who has come back from Moab, is selling the piece of land that belonged to our relative Elimelek. I thought I should bring the matter to your attention and suggest that you buy it in the presence of these seated here and in the presence of the elders of my people. If you will redeem it, do so. But if you will not, tell me, so I will know. For no one has the right to do it except you, and I am next in line." "I will redeem it," he said. Then Boaz said, "On the day you buy the land from Naomi, you also acquire Ruth the Moabite, the dead man's widow, in order to maintain the name of the dead with his property." Ruth 4:1-5 NIV

To redeem means to rescue, ransom, recover, fulfill, buyback, and liberate. As you read those words, do you see this is what Jesus accomplished at the cross of Calvary? He left everything in heaven because He was the only one with the power, humility, willingness, and sinlessness to redeem us.

When Boaz rescued Ruth, he foreshadowed what Jesus, our Redeemer, would do to save us.

Jesus redeemed us with His blood.

When Ruth left Boaz's presence, he did not let her go empty-handed. He gave her six measures of barley, which was approximately eighty-eight pounds. The six measures of barley are said to be a symbol of her destiny. Her lineage extended to six revered men, including David and the Messiah, Jesus. It's evident that with this gift, Boaz reassured her that all would be well. He would take care of the concerns she had. Ruth waited with expectation for Boaz to act. Let's look at the scripture below since it explains why Ruth was hopeful for the right outcome. Ruth was successful in her bid to win Boaz because, during that century, God had a plan to secure the widow's future through marriage.

If brothers are living together and one of them dies without a son, his widow must not marry outside the family. Her husband's brother shall take her and marry her and fulfill the duty of a brother-in-law to her. The first son she bears shall carry on the name of the dead brother so that his name will not be blotted out from Israel. However, if a man does not want to marry his brother's wife, she shall go to the elders at the town gate and say, "My husband's brother refuses to carry on his brother's name in Israel. He will not fulfill the duty of a brother-in-law to me." Then the elders of his town shall summon him and talk to him. If he persists in saying, "I do not want to marry her," his brother's widow shall go up to him in the presence of the elders, take off one

of his sandals, spit in his face and say, "This is what is done to the man who will not build up his brother's family line."
Deuteronomy 25:5-9 (NIV)

Have you ever thought about the significance of what Ruth did by uncovering Boaz's feet and lying down next to them? Ruth was in a desperate situation. She was poor. She was responsible for caring for Naomi. Ruth needed something drastic to change their situation. So, she did what was asked of her while uncertain about the outcome.

Some modern commentators will tell you what Naomi proposed, and what Ruth did was immodest, lacked integrity and honesty, and could have been misinterpreted. Even though the law allowed this marital opportunity, approaching it from this perspective was optional. Other commentators say Ruth essentially shamed him into redeeming her. One thing is for sure: God took what could have been an embarrassing situation and worked all of it for her good.

Women often talk about waiting on their Boaz, not fully realizing how Ruth acquired hers. Women generally prefer men not to feel obligated to them or constrained to marry, as such a dynamic is not a solid foundation for a relationship. Boaz, however, was ready to take up this responsibility because it was God's plan for their futures and not just Naomi's plan. I will dive deeper into this subject in an upcoming chapter.

As previously stated, the husband's brother was required to marry his brother's widow to keep his generational line intact. This marriage would ensure the deceased brother had a viable place in Israel's lineage. Ruth was purposeful in what she was asking Boaz to do. On the corner of a Jewish garment were fringes that were reminders for the people to keep the commandments of the Lord and not fulfill their desires. The Torah's teaching was the law God taught His people and covered the first five books of the Bible—Genesis, Exodus, Leviticus, Numbers, and Deuteronomy. It showed the people how to live. The Torah contained many of the commandments given by God.

Numbers 15:38-41 says this: *speak to the Israelites and say to them: 'Throughout the generations to come you are to make tassels on the corners of your garments, with a blue cord on each tassel. You will have these tassels to look at and so you will remember all the commands of the Lord, that you may obey them and not prostitute yourselves by chasing after the lusts of your own hearts and eyes. Then you will remember to obey all my commands and will be consecrated to your God. I am the Lord your God, who brought you out of Egypt to be your God. I am the Lord your God.'"*

When Boaz covered Ruth with his garment, he was following one of the commandments given by God. By observing this law, Boaz was following God's law of redemption. If he failed to honor the law, Boaz could be put to death. This decision was a serious commitment.

Boaz decided to free Ruth, and the barley he gave her was a down payment on what he pledged. He moved swiftly to honor his word because he would have had to keep re-supplying her if he took a long time.

Many women of today struggle with the men in their lives keeping their word. Some of us have heard from friends and loved ones how long it took some men to propose marriage. Some have shared how the delays for months to years impacted them.

Some women will stay in long-term relationships while hoping for a proposal and the marriage to occur. They might act as if it did not matter. But it mattered. Let me say this: people can get resentful when they are in these types of situations. To Boaz's credit, he understood time was of the essence and put action to his words.

We can learn many lessons from Boaz's actions. *Proverbs 18:22 says when a man finds a wife, he finds a good thing and obtains favor from the Lord.* What a powerful scripture. The man is to *find* the wife God has for him.

This scripture suggests he must search for her. It sounds like there will be other choices during the search. As he searches, he must consult God for insight and direction. When he finds her, his life will begin to improve. She is a good thing for him. She will add value to him. As a result of this union, he gains favor from the Lord.

It is essential to note the Bible tells you to find the one suitable for you. Interestingly, God had to say this because so many people pursue those unsuitable for them. These pursuits can cause significant conflicts in marriages. God guides our lives and orders our steps if we only listen and obey His directives instead of chasing our desires, wants, and fantasies.

Ruth had found favor with Boaz. Since he recognized the one who propositioned him was to be his wife, he hurried to secure this union. Boaz met with the other relative at the town gate, where business was generally transacted. He spoke to the relative about the relative buying Naomi's husband's property. The relative readily agreed until he learned Ruth was a part of the package. Like Onan, who was unwilling to produce an heir with Tamar, this relative was reluctant to take on the responsibility that came with Ruth. He was not interested in another wife. He was unwilling to give up his inheritance to another man's child.

Many people you meet are not called or qualified to be your mate. Only some people can go with you to the next level in your destiny. You cannot qualify your choices by praying the person changes. Wishing, hoping, and trying to change a person so they can become the right one is not God's plan for you.

You have to choose wisely. It is only with God's guidance that we can do this. You must allow the Holy Spirit to guide you to His choice. God has an excellent plan for your future, so don't get ahead of Him. Don't let impatience rule your decisions.

The relative passed his rights to buy the land to Boaz by removing his shoes. Removing his shoes was a sign of a legal transaction. Boaz gathered witnesses to confirm this transaction was legal. The elders who witnessed this transaction blessed Boaz and declared God would give him children through his marriage to Ruth.

A Son Is Born

After marrying Boaz, Ruth immediately conceived and gave birth to Obed. The women of the town blessed Naomi, saying God had given her a kinsman and began prophesying this son would restore her life. They declared this son was a reminder of Ruth's love for her.

Interesting, right? They equated the birth of Obed to Naomi instead of Ruth. They said this son was a gift to Naomi from God. They even named the baby Obed, meaning servant of God. He would nourish Naomi in old age. As Naomi took the baby into her arms, God, in His faithfulness, allowed milk to form in her breast even though she was past child-bearing age. It was Naomi's milk that was nourishment for this baby's life and not Ruth's. *This provision clearly shows although Naomi was past child-bearing age and thought God had abandoned her, He never did. He still had a plan for her even in her golden years.*

God gave Naomi a new purpose for her life. He gave her a son to replace the ones she lost. God removed the emptiness from her soul. Where she had previously felt useless and an outcast, He renewed her value and restored her status among the women. She could now lift her head and was no longer enshrouded with shame.

God raised her from the pit of grief and bitterness. He removed her guilt about going to Moab and losing her family. God shone a spotlight on her. I can imagine the stories the women of Naomi's century told about her being able to nurse this newborn baby in her old age. What a testament to God's unmatched power and faithfulness. God restored her completely.

Throughout these chapters, there is a glaring truth that we must address. The central focus of each chapter is Naomi. She was prominent throughout the entire narrative. As the story ends, Naomi, not Ruth, experiences promotion and receives praise. Ruth was the vessel God used to get His blessings through to Naomi, and she was indeed willing.

I am reminded of the story of Mary, the mother of Jesus. She was the vessel God used to get His gift, Jesus, into the earth to redeem humankind. After Jesus took center stage, Mary essentially faded into the background. I am aware man has created a massive religion around her life, but she was only the vessel that was willing and obedient. Remember, you only heard a little about Mary after Jesus took center stage and began His journey to the cross. She fulfilled a great destiny, but ultimately, Jesus was God's plan to redeem humanity.

God's plans far exceed ours. We have our plans, but they will never compare to His nor get us to the destinies He has in mind.

Jesus is the only faithful Redeemer. There was none before Him, and there is none after him. Romans 8:34 says Jesus is seated at God's right hand and interceding for us. Listen: Every other man-made deity has died and is still dead. Only Jesus rose from the grave and is very much alive today. He reigns as King of kings and Lord of lords because God has given Him the highest place of honor in heaven. We also know He is alive because He lives in us and guides our lives daily.

We will one day spend eternity with Him.

In some religions, Jesus is still depicted as hanging on the cross. He is no longer there. Jesus rose with all power and authority in His hands because He conquered death, hell, and the grave and now reigns supreme. *He was battered, broken, and bruised on the way to the cross. Yet even in that horrific condition, He was unstoppable. He is our perfect example of overcoming brokenness and remaining unstoppable in the difficult situations of our lives.*

He is our Kinsman-Redeemer.

CHAPTER 7

Rest For The Weary

Has life wearied you? Are you worn out? So many people have experienced hard, painful times and are overburdened and worn by them. It is almost impossible to find anyone who has not experienced some hardship. Some are due to health, finances, the death of loved ones, or simply not having the means to take care of their daily needs.

Naomi and Ruth faced these same hardships. The loss of her husband and her sons weighed heavily on Naomi. Their deaths caused her profound grief, and she wanted to give up on life. Journeying home, Naomi was both tired and embittered by the circumstances of her life.

Ruth was grieving many losses—her husband, family, home, a comfortable environment with her family and within her nation. She left everything to face an uncertain future. Ruth was in a difficult situation but pressed on. She was focused and unstoppable.

You might agree with Naomi. Often, we are unsure what

caused the magnitude of struggles in our lives. Sometimes, we look at others around us and wonder why they have it so much better than we do. They don't appear to face the same level of difficulties as us. These are often assumptions because things can appear a certain way, but reality is different. Please consider the people who seem to have abundant wealth and prosperity but cannot fully enjoy it because they are in health battles or other struggles.

Life appears to be so unequal, right? It is unequal because of sin and the choices people have made. We have used our free will and made decisions that have caused devastation in our lives. Some people are abundantly blessed in their health and finances, while others face daily struggles. God did not design it that way. Did you know God has provided an abundance of everything needed to sustain all eight-plus billion people on Earth? Yes, He has.

The level of poverty that Naomi, Ruth, and the others working in the fields experience was not by God's design but because of a corrupt world system. The poverty we see in the United States, the wealthiest country on Earth, is astounding and unthinkable. The poverty we see around the world is truly unbelievable when we think about all the provisions God has put into the Earth. We sing songs that depict God as a good Father, and He is. A good father takes care of the needs of his children. God has done exactly that. Philippians 4:19 says, *but my God will supply all your needs according to his riches in glory in Christ Jesus.*

God sent His Son, Jesus, to die in our place to redeem us so we can experience abundance in all areas of life. One of my favorite scriptures is 3 John 1:2, where the Father tells us, *"Beloved, I wish above all else that you prosper and be in health even as your soul prospers."* Do you see it?

His wish for you, above everything else, is for you to prosper.

How? In your body, mind, soul, and spirit. He wants you to be healed and made whole.

Wholeness means—unbroken, restored, undiminished, and abounding with good health. He said He 'wished' for this. A wish is to express a strong desire or hope that you can obtain the things you need. Wish also means to crave or to want something desperately. The Father sincerely wishes that you prosper in every area of your life. Since He is God, why does He not simply make this happen for me?

The simple answer is that humankind was given the ability to choose.

Choice started in the Garden of Eden. God gave man life and allowed him to choose his way. Our choices determine our outcome. As we review our lives, we can all attest to this. Humankind ultimately does not always make the right choices, keeping us in this vicious cycle of struggle and suffering. We have been in a life-and-death battle ever since the fall in the Garden of Eden. God, in His abundant grace, has helped us to find hope and healing even when our choices lead us to endure pain and hardships.

Naomi's husband's choices had taken them away from their homeland. Naomi lost almost everything and was devastated. Despite Naomi and her husband's bad decisions, God turned it around and brought her a good outcome. She gained a daughter-in-law, Ruth, who stood by her through the darkest times in her life.

Even though their choice to go to Moab was not what God wanted for their lives, He still stepped in, helped her recover, and gave her a new life. Romans 8:28 says *all things work together for good to them who love God, to them who are the called according to his purpose.* Naomi and her family loved God; they stepped away from His protection, and she suffered severe consequences.

Notice, even in this, God gave her a remnant in the Earth. He gave her a grandson who would remain by her side after the loss of her sons. As a result of Ruth's marriage to Boaz, Naomi's family lineage would not end. Ruth was the seed God used to bring her into a place of restoration.

Even when we make wrong choices, God still guides and helps us. He never deserts us or leaves us broken, hopeless, or devastated.

Come to Me

Naomi went home. She went back to where she had left God. When we face difficulties, we often lament that God has left us. Naomi lamented this. God did not leave Naomi; she left Him. She returned broken, but God was there, ready, and available to pick up the pieces of her life and to give her a new beginning.

Think about your life. Do you, at times, believe God has left you? If you answered yes, be assured He has not. Maybe you have wandered away from His protection because of your choices. It is easy for me and others to blame God when we struggle. It is easy to reason that since He is God, He should prevent these bad things from happening to us. Naomi felt precisely like this.

Unfortunately, we often blame the One who genuinely desires the best for us. Let me repeat it: God wants the very best life for you. He wants you to be filled with hope, joy, and peace. God wants to flood your heart and life with His abundant supplies. Numerous scriptures in the Bible affirm and support this truth. Let's look at a great reminder in Matthew 11.

"Come to me, all you who are weary and burdened, and I will give you rest. Take my yoke upon you and learn from me, for I am gentle and humble in heart, and you will find rest for your souls. For my yoke is easy and my burden is light."
Matthew 11:28-30 (NIV)

Jesus tells you 'to come to Him all who are weary.' Do you find your way to Jesus when weariness tries to overtake you? When you go to Him, He says He will give you rest. I need rest, how about you?

In chapter one, I shared the journey of my mother, Gwen, before she went home to the Lord. As I mentioned in that same chapter, I will share the painful journey of my dad's sickness, his struggles, hardships, weariness, and the ultimate rest my stepmom and family received from the Lord.

Our story reflects many of your stories centered around health crises. I often tell my staff that our hospital system is one of the largest organizations in the USA. Whether it is the children's hospitals or the ones for adults, the parking lots are always almost filled with vehicles. What a tragedy this is. So many people are sick and struggling with pain, and some situations are extreme. It is hard not to find people who do not know someone battling cancer, Alzheimer's, diabetes, or heart disease. This list is unending. Jesus understands this suffering. Freedom from suffering is part of our salvation that He died for.

Salvation in Greek is Sozo. It means to heal, save, deliver, make well, make whole, and set free. Jesus paid it all for us at Calvary. We must take His Word and declare its promises over our health and that of our loved ones. You may think, "I don't know the scriptures or have time to do this as I care for my loved ones." Let me say—this is a must so Jesus can intervene in your situation. You may be saying you have declared His Word, and you are still sick, or your loved ones still died.

In some cases, this is true. God's Word has the power to change your current situation in an instant. As hard as this is to say or understand, death, going home to Jesus, is also a part of healing. Revelation 21:4 tells us with Jesus, we will no longer mourn, cry, or endure pain. Truth is—your loved ones who have died, if they had a relationship with Jesus, are now pain-free. In His presence, they have experienced ultimate healing.

The story of my dad, Octavious, will give you some
insight into God's mercy for all His children. God does
give us rest in our weariness.

My dad began battling Dementia/Alzheimer's approximately three years before it became severe. He would forget
things like where he placed his van keys, which progressed to
other things he could not recall. We recognized the severity of
the disease when he walked out of the doctor's office while
waiting for his wife. He was lost for many hours. It was only
prayer and the mercy of God that brought him home. From
that moment onward, the disease progressed at a rapid pace. My
stepmom, Patsy, as his primary caregiver, suffered intense
emotional pain as he declined before her eyes.

During one conversation with my stepmom, Patsy, she was
extremely devastated and was weeping profusely. She had been
grieving for many months and years. During this conversation,
my heart was breaking as I heard her sob. I had been praying
daily for God to heal my dad. I trust He would answer me. I
know many others were also praying for him. My dad had lost a
significant amount of weight because he had stopped eating and
could not stay awake.

It was evident to us he was about to pass. As I listened to my
stepmom, I realized if he died, she would be devastated and
unable to manage. She needed time to accept this significant
loss and find peace with the situation.

Realizing this, I asked her, 'Mom, do you have my prayer

book?" She was puzzled and annoyed that in the midst of her weeping, I would be asking about a book. I knew that in the book, *I Must Pray*, was a prayer for healing filled with the scriptures. I was absolutely confident as we prayed God's Word over him; it would work and produce results. She had the book, and I instructed her to open it to page 134 and declare the prayer over Dad each morning, adding his name where indicated. I told her to tell the two helpers to do the same thing at noon and before my dad's bedtime. She said she would.

A few days later, I called to check on her. She was still weeping profusely, and Dad was declining fast. I asked if she had been declaring the prayer with God's Word over him. She had not begun. I became irritated with her and grabbed the book from my bookshelf, determined to get this started. I believed the scriptures would make a change in his life. I asked her to take the phone to Dad, but she said he could not stay awake and would not hear me.

I firmly told her I was not speaking to his mind but to his spirit. She took the phone to him. I prayed the prayer over him. I then instructed the workers to do the same. From that day forward, I called my dad each morning and prayed over him while the workers did the same throughout the day. My stepmom and many others also prayed often for him.

Within a month, changes began to happen. Dad was able to stay awake longer. He then started to eat small amounts of food. As the months passed, Dad could get out of bed by himself and would often shock them when he popped up unexpectedly. He began to speak again.

Over the months, the changes in him and his mobility were very significant, surprising many who previously thought he was about to die. We continued the daily prayers. Dad got out of the house with his caregivers' help and visited family and friends. He started giving gifts to people as he had previously done. He made jokes and laughed at our jokes. His short and long-term memories did not return, but his cognizant abilities did. His wife would often remark that after a conversation with him, she would walk away from him, forgetting that he had Dementia/Alzheimer's.

She still grieved the loss of their relationship and all the responsibilities she now had, but for a season, God lifted some of her burdens and gave her a measure of peace. For one year, my dad improved. At Christmas time, he gathered with the family for dinner as in previous years and ate a significant amount of food. He had improved so significantly that he could participate in the festivities.

As we entered the new year, Dad began to decline. We knew he would not recover this time, but we continued praying until the end in case God provided another miracle.

God gave his wife, Patsy, and us time to accept his passing and to be ready to move forward without him. This additional time was such a loving demonstration of God's abundant love and mercy for him and us. One year after God began the journey of healing and restoring him, Dad went home to his great reward. We are thankful for God's mercy and compassion toward us.

I want to report that even though the funeral was painful and difficult for us, especially my stepmom, God was with us each step of the way. My stepmom misses him but decided that she would not stop living. She faithfully served Dad, and now it was her time to heal and then move forward to a full life without him.

She has found rest from her labor and is beginning to enjoy each day. My stepmom is helping others whose loved ones are battling devastating diseases and life's struggles. Supporting others is helping her in her season of grieving. She is living proof God helps us in our time of need. My dad is home with our Savior, Jesus, and is now free from sickness and pain.

What great hope we as Believers have in Jesus Christ.

We know Dad is in our future, not our past, because He invited Jesus to live in his heart. He is home free.

The Bible does not tell us how Naomi's husband and children died. Were they sick, or was it sudden? We also do not know what difficulties Ruth endured before and during the death of her husband. Deaths happened centuries ago, just like they do today. Like my stepmom, their grief was profound. We mourn, cry, and grieve. Then, we pick up the pieces and learn to live with the losses. For many people, this is extremely hard. We don't have any other choice but to TRUST God to walk with us during the hard seasons.

I want to remind you of a truth I shared with you earlier. There is Only one person we ultimately cannot live without—Jesus. Death separates you from your loved ones. In many cases, people will heal and move forward to live productive lives and, sometimes, create great purposes from their losses.

Like my stepmom, Patsy, people's grief can be profound. They miss their loved ones, but life must continue. Know this —if Jesus ever leaves you, you will be forever lost and without hope. You and I cannot live without Jesus.

In Ruth 1:13, you can hear Naomi's weariness with her life

as she tells her daughters-in-law to return to their family. She told them the Lord's hand was turned against her. These were such hopeless words. She was tired of all her loads, weights, and burdens.

You might identify with her. You are at the end of your rope and feel like you are sinking deeper into despair. Naomi was in despair. Ruth was also in a battle with her losses, but she found enough strength within herself to help raise Naomi's hope. Ruth gave Naomi a reason to keep putting one foot in front of the other.

As Naomi headed home, she had help on every side. She could only see Ruth, her helper, walking steadily beside her. She could not see that God was with her, close to her. He is always close to the brokenhearted. He was ready, willing, and available to give her a new, brighter future.

In Matthew 11:28-30, Matthew talks to us about being overloaded and overburdened. He tells us Jesus wants us to come and unburden ourselves to Him. The enemy has worn us out with all the cares of our lives and even what we see unfolding in the world. Jesus invites all of us to come and release the cares to Him.

We are not built or equipped to carry these burdens. They are wearing us down. These burdens are too heavy and exhausting for us. Jesus wants you to cease, desist, and refrain from weariness. He says to take His yoke upon you, for His yoke is easy, and His burdens are light. Be deliberate about accepting this offer of freedom. You must invite Him to be the burden-bearer.

The word 'yoke' in Greek is Zugos. This word describes a wooden yoke that joins two animals together to combine their strength and pull the load together because it is too difficult for one by them self. Yoking the animals together makes the team inseparable. The team is stronger together than they are apart. The animals must pull together and head in the same direction. Going in opposite directions would not get them to the desired destination.

You are stronger when yoked with Jesus than you are by yourself. You must decide to go in the direction He is leading you. Remember, He knows the plans He has for you. They are plans to bless you and not to harm you. To give you hope and a future (Jeremiah 29:11). He knows what He is doing. Therefore, you can trust Him. He wants you to make a predetermination and a deliberate decision to yoke yourself to Him so He can carry your load and pull you along until you get to your future and the blessings He has in store for you.

When you are joined with Him, you are unbeatable. You become a conqueror. You gain the victory. You cannot fail, nor will you lose your way in the struggles against weariness. Jesus makes your burden lighter and your load easier to carry.

This example speaks to what happened with Naomi and Ruth. Ruth yoked herself to Naomi so she was not carrying her load alone and vice-versa. As she journeyed home, Naomi discovered that with Ruth by her side, her burdens and steps became lighter because she had support to pull her through each difficult day. Ecclesiastes 4:9-10 says *two are better than one, because they have a good return for their labor: If either of them falls down, one can help the other up. But pity anyone who falls and has no one to help them up. Also, if two lie down together, they will keep warm. But how can one keep warm alone? Though one may be overpowered, two can defend themselves. A cord of three strands is not quickly broken.*

What a powerful scripture. God has given us the solution for our victory. Yoke yourself to Him. Stay connected no matter what you are facing. You have helped on every side because

Jesus is right beside you. You have a defender in Him. A cord of three strands is not quickly broken—you, Jesus, and the Holy Spirit are unbeatable and unstoppable. Nothing can ever separate you from the deep love and care Jesus has for you. Hold tightly to Him, and your victory and breakthroughs will be assured.

Let's explore some scriptures that will encourage you if you are in a season of weariness. Remember, the Word of God has the power to change your life and situations. It can lift you above the pain and hardships life has imposed.

Scriptures to Combat Weariness

.

- Galatians 6:9 - And let us not grow weary in doing good, for in due season we will reap, if we do not give up.
- 2 Thessalonians 3:13 - As for you, brothers, do not grow weary in doing good.
- Psalm 68:9 - You gave abundant showers, O God; you refreshed your weary inheritance.
- Psalm 119:28 - My soul is weary with sorrow; strengthen me according to your Word.
- Proverbs 25:25 - Like cold water to a weary soul is good news from a distant land.
- Isaiah 57:15 - For I satisfy the weary ones and refresh everyone who languishes.
- Isaiah 40:31 - Yet those who wait for the Lord will gain new strength.

My prayer for you is you gain new strength in the painful journeys of life. Jesus will help you overcome and live victoriously. With Him on your side, you are unstoppable. Remain steady. He will guide your steps and take you from glory to glory and faith to faith (2 Timothy 2:10).

CHAPTER 8

Jesus, Our Redeemer

Believers in Jesus Christ understand what it means to be redeemed. We know Jesus is the one who has redeemed us. The word redeem in Hebrew is 'ga'al', which means to regain possession of something or someone by repayment. It is to buy back something that was lost. In Greek, it means to deliver, redeem, act as a kinsman, and avenge.

Redeem implies the deliverance of a people. This is what Jesus did after Adam and Eve sinned in the Garden of Eden, relinquishing their authority and rights to the devil. Jesus stepped in to repurchase us from the clutches of the evil one. Jesus shed His blood on Calvary to restore us to the right relationship with God, our Father.

Hebrews 9:22 says that without the shedding of blood, there is no forgiveness of sin. Without Jesus' death on the cross, you would not be free or restored to God. Jesus is our great High Priest, and He shed His blood once and for all to free you.

No earthly priest can present your sins before God to secure your forgiveness. You will no longer have to wait once a year for the animal sacrifices to be offered to God as repentance for your sins. Because of Jesus, you now have access to His presence day and night.

Hebrews 1:16 tells us to come boldly to the throne of grace to obtain mercy and find grace to help us in times of need. You can boldly go to God because Jesus provided access to Him through His death, burial, and resurrection. What a wonderful gift God has given to us. This gift is available to everyone. You only have to believe and accept His great sacrifice.

In Genesis 14:18-20, we are introduced to Melchizedek, the king of Salem and priest of the Most High God, El Elyon. El Elyon is one of the names of God, and it means "The Most High God." Melchizedek is introduced to us when he brought bread and wine to bless Abraham after Abraham returned from rescuing Lot, his nephew, who was held prisoner during a battle between various kings in the region.

After Melchizedek blessed him, Abraham gave tithes to Him. The tithe he gave is significant because many arguments today exist about who we should pay tithes to. Tithes are not paid to the church or the Pastor but to God. Abraham recognized Melchizedek was not a mere human being but someone special from God, so he paid tithe to him after successfully rescuing Lot.

Hebrews 7:3 tells us Melchizedek had no mother or father or no genealogical line. He had no beginning of days nor end of life, and he continues as a priest forever.

Hebrews 6:20 tells us Jesus is a high priest after the order of Melchizedek. He is a more extraordinary high priest than the Levites priests of the Old Testament.

Jesus is said to be a priest after the order of Melchizedek because Jesus is a priest forever. Jesus and Melchizedek are

God's Priests. They were not descendants of Aaron and were not qualified for the Jewish priesthood under the laws of Moses.

In the old covenant, the high priest made sacrifices in the Tabernacle once a year for his and the Israelites' sins. The high priest would enter the holy place, sacrifice an unblemished animal, and then apply the blood to forgive his sin and the people's sins (Hebrews 9:7).

Our great High Priest, Jesus, redeemed us.

In Chapter 6, I shared that by rescuing Ruth, Boaz acted as a kinsman-redeemer because he paid the ultimate price for her. He bought her, married her, and restored her life. This beautiful example reflects what Jesus Christ did for us. Jesus is our Kinsman-Redeemer. Take a journey with me as we explore the sacrifices of Jesus, our Redeemer.

Jesus Gave ALL!

As we study the Old Testament, we see clear examples in the many recorded prophesies about Jesus being the Son of God. The prophet Isaiah shared approximately fifty prophesies about the birth, death, and resurrection of Jesus. He pointed us to the truth that Jesus is the Savior of the world. The prophets of old knew Jesus would be the Redeemer of humanity. Therefore, the example of Boaz as the kinsman-redeemer who bought Ruth out of slavery and poverty reflects our one faithful Redeemer, Jesus. As we look at the life of Boaz, he is a foreshadowing of what Jesus would become, our True Redeemer.

As previously mentioned, the first thing Boaz did the morning after Ruth lay at his feet was to redeem her. The first thing Jesus did when He rose from the grave was to redeem us.

Boaz fulfilled the law by freeing Ruth from slavery. Jesus freed all of humankind from slavery to sin and delivered us from bondage. Boaz purchased Ruth for eighty-eight pounds of barley as a sign of his commitment to her. Jesus sacrificed His life and spilled His blood to redeem and reunite us with God, our Father. Jesus provided a way for us to spend eternity with the Father, Son, and Holy Spirit. Only a blood relative could free Ruth from slavery. No one but Jesus Christ could redeem us from sin because He is God's only sinless, spotless lamb.

There are no substitutes for Jesus. He will forever be our only Redeemer. His shed blood relates Him to us because only in His human nature could His blood be shed to forgive our sins and to restore us to the right relationship with God. His redemption gives us total security in Him. We have an eternal guarantee of being eternally free because of His sacrifice.

Think about what you just read. Can you feel the depth of the Father's love for you? His love caused Him to give His best —Jesus, His only Son, in exchange for you. I say this often—if you were the only person on planet Earth, God would have still sent Jesus to die that horrible death just for you, alone. Jesus' death reflects the depth of His love for you. How great is the love of the Father extended to you and me and to all who will respond to this great love. To understand the magnitude of His love, we must look at what Jesus gave up in Heaven to come to Earth and redeem us.

Emptied His Heavenly Status

Therefore, if you have any encouragement from being united with Christ, if any comfort from his love, if any common sharing in the Spirit, if any tenderness and compassion, then make my joy complete by being like-minded, having the same love, being one in spirit and of one mind. Do nothing out of selfish ambition or vain conceit. Rather, in humility value others above yourselves, not looking to your own interests but each of you to the interests of the others. In your relationships with one another, have the same mindset as Christ Jesus: Who, being in very nature God, did not consider equality with God something to be used to his own advantage; rather, he made himself nothing by taking the very nature of a servant, being made in human likeness. And being found in appearance as a man, he humbled himself by becoming obedient to death— even death on a cross! Therefore God exalted him to the highest place and gave him the name that is above every name, that at the name of Jesus, every knee should bow, in Heaven and on earth and under the earth, and every tongue acknowledge that Jesus Christ is Lord, to the glory of God the Father.

Philippians 2:1-11 (NIV)

To come to earth and redeem us, Jesus, being God's Son,

had to empty Himself of all the status He had in Heaven. From the throne of Heaven, where He lived for many centuries, to the cross of Calvary, He set aside His glory and majesty to become our Redeemer. The Bible tells us Jesus is Emanuel, which means God with us. He is Yahweh, our Salvation. In 1 Samuel 17:45, God is known as Yahweh Tevaot. This name implies He is the God of the armies of Israel. We are introduced to Him when David faced off against the Philistine in the name of the Lord Almighty. His presence came down amid the Israelites as they faced their enemies.

Yahweh is God's covenant name. A biblical covenant is an agreement between God and His people. God makes covenant promises to us, and when we align ourselves with Him, we obtain the promises. God keeps His covenant with man. When Adam and Eve sinned and sold us into slavery to the devil, His covenant was to redeem us. Jesus is God incarnate in human form.

Incarnate means a deity who has embodied human form. Jesus became flesh so He could relate to us. Throughout the Bible, Jesus is fully revealed as the Father. In John 10:30, Jesus tells us that He and the Father are one.

Let's look at a few other scriptures that speak of Jesus' deity:

- John 5:18 – He is equal with God.
- John 8:58 – He is the Yahweh of the Old Testament.
- John 15:5 – He existed before the world was formed.
- John 14:9 – He says, he that has seen me has seen the Father.
- Mark 2:10 – He has the power to forgive sins.

- Mark 3:11 – Demons trembled before Him and
  acknowledged He is the Most-High God.
- John 14:16 – Jesus says, I am the way, the truth, and
  the life. No one comes to the Father except
  through me.
- Matthew 28:20 – He says I am with you always.

The above scripture references and many more throughout
the Bible tell us that Jesus is Lord and Savior. Before He came as
our Kinsman-Redeemer, Jesus went through a complete transformation. He emptied Himself of His status and became a
baby who lived in one of God's earthy creations for nine
months.

Ponder that for a moment. As a baby, He needed His mother's help to survive. In Philippians 2:1-6, we find what is known
as the seven-fold humbling of Jesus. As you study the passage,
you will see the steps Jesus took from the throne to the cross
and from the cross back to the throne.

Let's explore the first six verses of Philippians 2 so we can
walk in Jesus' footsteps.

- The Bible says Jesus was in the nature of God but
  did not consider equality with God something to be
  grasped.
- He made Himself nothing.
- He became a servant.
- He became human in appearance.
- He humbled Himself and obediently went to death
  on the cross.

As you read those statements, can you see the humility in

each step He took to ransom and redeem us? So, what did Jesus give up?

- He laid aside His glory.
- He shed His divine nature.
- He, who had always existed, walked away from that existence.

He was in the form of God (Morphe in Greek) but relinquished it.

The Bible tells us Jesus is God in human flesh. He assumed a human form, relinquishing His divine nature, splendor, majesty, and, ultimately, His power and authority to establish a connection with humanity. Had Jesus come to Earth in the form He existed in Heaven, we could not have handled His heavenly form or related to Him. His magnificent presence would be too powerful for us; therefore, He re-clothed Himself in a manner we could accept.

The Bible says, 'He made Himself of no reputation.' This means He did not consider His good name, status, or reputation as He humbled Himself to die in our place.

Jesus emptied Himself. He poured it all out. When He gave up His heavenly status to redeem man, He deprived Himself of all His glory and worship. He temporarily relinquished all power and completely changed His outward appearance to live among us. He willingly, deliberately, and ultimately released all of His glorious attributes so He could relate to us.

Jesus took on the form of a servant, which means He became flesh. Jesus reached out of His eternal existence and grabbed hold of humanity.

Listen: He came into the world He created and became what He created. The Creator became one of us, a human being with all our feelings, aspirations, desires, and hopes. He was just like us, yet He was sinless.

The Bible tells us that Jesus feels what we feel in becoming like us. He has given us many examples in the Bible of how we can be victorious and overcome all the painful, challenging obstacles we face daily.

Jesus enslaved Himself, utterly opposite of what He was, so that He could fit in with humankind. His sole purpose was to reunite us with God. He was like a man in every way. He was tempted, tested, and tried as you are but did not sin. Out of His deep love for us, a love beyond compare, Jesus left the majesty of Heaven and its glorious splendor to enter broken humanity because love beckoned Him.

Jesus was Fashioned as a Man

The scripture says Jesus was 'fashioned as a man.' Being fashioned is an interesting choice of words to describe Jesus. It is not what we consider fashion to be. This word carries a greater meaning. Fashion in Greek is *schema* and is used to depict a king who exchanges his kingly garments for a brief period for the clothing of a beggar.

God, in the form of His Son, Jesus, laid aside His radiant glory and took on dust, our form. He exchanged His royal robes for human flesh. He humbled Himself, becoming obedient to death on the cross.

Fashioned means—he became lowly. He willing stooped low to repurchase us. He divested Himself of all splendor and put Himself under man's authority. Surrendering was not pleasurable, but Jesus did it anyway because His one focus was us.

Jesus was not excited to follow man-made earthly rules, but He came knowing this was one of His purposes—allowing men to beat Him and then hang Him on a cross. Why? Without His shed blood, you would not be experiencing the freedom you have right now. He suffered that miserable, horrible, painful death for the sole purpose of restoring us to His Father, God.

We are saved because He gave His life in exchange for us.

Let's return to Boaz and Ruth. Ruth needed help, rescue, food, and shelter. She was out in the fields doing hard, back-breaking work. God could have allowed her to keep working hard to sustain herself, but His plans for us are always better and far exceed ours. God redeemed Ruth and Naomi from a life of lack, pain, hardships, disappointments, and continued hurts by allowing Boaz to marry Ruth.

Do you now see why Boaz was a foreshadowing of Jesus?

Jesus rescued us just as Boaz rescued Ruth. Jesus' rescue was even more complete. He provided full restoration. His sacrifice was more profound, painful, and costly for Him, offering us more significant benefits, including eternal life.

His impact on our lives is permanent. Boaz's redemption provided temporary relief throughout Ruth's life. Jesus' redemption provides lasting relief, peace, safety, and hope for every day to come—all our tomorrows. There is no pain, lack, hurts, or suffering in eternity—nothing to devastate your life. Jesus has lifted us from death to life just as Boaz lifted Ruth out of poverty. Truly, redemption is the greatest gift of love.

Are you celebrating what Jesus accomplished for you on Calvary? Come with me as we journey through His death, burial, and resurrection.

His Journey to the Cross

When we reflect on Jesus' sacrifice, we may not think about His journey to the cross. From the Garden of Gethsemane to Calvary, Jesus suffered. First, Roman's crosses were made as a "T" and weighed one hundred pounds. The Roman soldiers would walk the person carrying their cross through the streets, and a herald would proclaim their crimes. Jesus was crucified outside of the city of Jerusalem; therefore, as He carried His cross, people followed Him and heard the made-up crimes.

As Jesus struggled to carry the cross on His broken, battered body, He stumbled often and fell. His body was torn to shreds.

Blood drenched His face. He was marred beyond recognition. It is, therefore, surprising that the soldiers, who were brutal and inhumane, recognized He was unable to carry the cross up Golgotha's hill. They grabbed a man named Simon of Cyrene to carry the cross for Jesus.

Think about that for a moment. Jesus needed help to carry His cross/burden the same way we need Him to carry our burdens. This is why He tells us to cast our burdens on Him. Jesus' need for help speaks of humility. In His greatest struggles, He needed help to get to His destiny, the cross. He accepted help when it was offered to Him.

What a lesson for us. We must take the help Jesus sends us as we struggle with the burdens and cares of life. You will need Jesus' help to get to your destiny and finish the earthly assignment God gave you.

Simon and the rest of the people were spectators to the humiliation that the Romans heaped on Jesus. The people all around Jesus were shouting, "Crucify Him." I must speculate. Was Simon one of those who yelled those words, or did He feel compassion for the pain and suffering Jesus was enduring? Whatever his position, he was commanded to carry Jesus' load —the one-hundred-pound cross on his back. The one difference was that his back was not broken or blooded from the thirty-nine stripes, as was Jesus' back.

Simon was not asked to carry Jesus' cross but was 'compelled' to do so. The soldiers did not give him a choice to say no to this assignment. The word compelled means he was ordered, pressured, and forcefully made to carry the cross. Think about that momentarily and then compare it to what Jesus did.

Jesus was not compelled, ordered, pressured, or forcefully made to die on Calvary. He *chose* this path. Jesus said *yes* to this death. He surrendered to the Father's desire to bring us back into intimate relationships and fellowship with Him. Jesus knew that our sins would not be forgiven without the shedding of His blood (Hebrews 9:22).

———

He did it for you and me.

———

Truly a reason to pause and say "Thank you."

———

Matthew, Mark, and Luke share the same account of Simon, who became a part of Jesus' journey and history without planning to. Cyrene, where Simon resided, was a coastal town on the Mediterranean Sea and had a population of five thousand people. The Greeks made Cyrene a trade outpost.

Acts 2:10 tells how the people of Cyrene heard Peter preach in their language after Jesus rose from death. Do you think Simon was one of the ones who heard Peter's message? It is possible. It is also possible Simon became a believer after witnessing Jesus' death on the cross he carried. When anyone meets Jesus, their lives are forever changed. I am convinced Simon was never the same after his encounter with Jesus.

Crucifixion means punishment meted out to criminals by the Roman soldiers. It also means to be impaled, hung up, and to be publicly displayed. Crucifixion was intended to bring further humiliation to the criminals. Crucifixion was one of the most merciless, inhumane, and despicable deaths known to man during that century.

When the Roman soldiers crucified criminals, they hung a sign with the person's crime over their heads. They did the same with Jesus. The sign read—"King of the Jews." The Jewish leaders hated it. The soldiers would not relent and change the wording on the sign.

As Jesus hung on the cross, He was offered vinegar mingled with gall. According to Jewish law, if a man was to be crucified, he could request a narcotic to alleviate the pain. Gall was a type of painkiller. Jesus was offered this two times, once before the crucifixion and once while on the cross. He refused both times, choosing to suffer the pain because He was fully consumed with this cup given to Him by God, the Father.

He Died in Our Place

Jesus died in your place—He died for you. God sent Jesus His best gift for you. His sacrifice shows how much God wanted to reunite with you, restore you to His family, and resume uninterrupted fellowship with you. Love laid down His life to redeem and restore you to God.

Love is Jesus.

Jesus was laid on the cross with arms outstretched once He reached the place where He was to be crucified. A soldier drove five-inch nails through His wrist and into the crossbeam. His feet were positioned together, one on the other, so the soldiers could drive nails between the bones to prevent tearing. A rope hoisted Jesus, and the cross beam dropped into its slot.

Take a moment and imagine the agony He endured. Consider how the sudden movement jerked His hands and feet. Hanging by His hands and feet, most of His weight was on His arms. This caused His arms to be pulled from their socket. To me, this pain is unimaginable.

I previously had a 'frozen shoulder,' and the pain was so unbearable I could not function. A friend told me she had the same issue, and in her opinion, it was the worst pain she had ever experienced, including childbirth.

It is hard to imagine or explain the pain Jesus endured while hanging on the cross. No words can describe what Jesus suffered for us. The amazing thing is that Jesus endured all this in complete silence, never once crying out as He suffered.

As Jesus hung on the cross, dying, four soldiers divided His clothes among themselves. His coat, the Tallit, with fringes, was expensive and seamless, so they decided not to tear it. While He hung dying on a cross for them, the soldiers cast lots for it. As Jesus breathed some of His last breaths, they played games over who would own His clothes.

I want to close this chapter with an observation. Many people wear beautiful crosses. These crosses are meant to remind us of Jesus' sacrifice. Many of these crosses are empty— Jesus is no longer on the cross. He was buried, rose again, and is seated at the right hand of God, interceding for us (Romans 8:34).

The cross of Jesus was not beautiful at all. It was shocking, horrifying, dreadful, terrible, awful, revolting, sickening, and indeed a stomach-turning sight. I wish I had more words to describe it. It was inhumane. Compared to what Jesus suffered, the crosses we wear are beautiful, comforting, and reminders of His sacrifice for us.

As we wear these beautiful crosses that bring the promises of Jesus close to our hearts, know there was nothing beautiful about what Jesus endured or suffered on that Roman cross to win your freedom. As you often reflect on His sacrifice, remember there will never be anything attractive about the horrific nature of His death other than He chose this death for you. You and I have reasons to be deeply ***thankful.***

Boaz redeemed Ruth without suffering or dying. He received an immediate reward: a loving and supportive wife and companion. Proverbs 18:22 tells us when a man finds a wife, he finds a good thing and obtains favor from the Lord. Boaz found a good thing, gained favor, and gained a son. Jesus' redemption of us was far different. He had to give His life to earn ours. He is the one and only Son given in exchange for us.

Before gaining His reward, He suffered, was killed, and then buried. He went into hell and took back our authority that Adam gave away to the devil. Jesus then rose triumphantly with all power in His hands and at His disposal. He reentered Heaven to receive His reward—a position of most incredible honor next to His Father, God.

Jesus once again is receiving His worship, glory, adoration, and the reverence that He previously received. Revelation 19:16 tells us about Jesus. *On his robe and on his thigh, he has this name written: King of kings and Lord of lords.* Jesus has received His rewards for redeeming us. Are you grateful for your redemption? I am grateful.

Through His sacrifice, He has made you unstoppable.

CHAPTER 9

New Beginnings

To me, a fresh start means a new beginning. We all like do-overs. A do-over gives us opportunities to start again after we may have made some missteps and suffered some losses. People who have lost loved ones, especially spouses, genuinely have to start again. They must revamp their lives, make decisions independently, and chart a new course. Some have lost children and find it challenging to think about the future without them.

Many in our society find themselves in this place of new beginnings. People die due to sickness/diseases, accidents, shootings, etc. All these unexpected life events have pushed many people into new beginnings.

My parents experienced this with the death of their oldest son. For many years after his death, my stepmom worked hard to deal with her loss. My dad did not; he buried his emotions.

Years after his son's death, and when he developed Dementia and Alzheimer's, we realized this trauma and other challenging issues in his life impacted him more significantly than we realized. In retrospect, if he had received counseling, it would have helped him deal with these heartbreaking issues. He would have found a measure of peace with his losses. My dad did not experience a fresh start or a new beginning after his significant loss.

As families grieve their losses, they strive to find new beginnings. Ruth and Naomi experienced this. After their tragic losses, they began a new journey—physically and spiritually into an unknown future. God guided and provided for them when they arrived at their new beginnings. God will also guide and help you as you begin again.

Naomi's New Beginning

In chapter 6, we briefly touched on the amazing miracle God did for Naomi after Obed, Ruth's son, was born. God caused milk to form in her breast so she could nurse him even though she was past childbearing age. He gave her a new beginning, a fresh start, a new lease on life. Naomi had a new purpose and a reason to keep living. Instead of withering away in grief, sorrow, and bitterness, she was given a reason to get up each day and to be hopeful.

Let me reiterate her struggles as we briefly walk in her shoes. She had despaired that God had abandoned her. She felt He did not care she had lost her husband and sons. Naomi thought there was no more reason to live. As she prepared to return home, she was embarrassed to face her extended family, neighbors, and friends. Yet, God was planning a future filled with blessings and provisions for her.

I am reminded of Jeremiah 29:11, which says, *I know the plans I have for you declares the Lord, plans to prosper you and not to harm you, plans to give you hope and a future.* This new birth, this new beginning, was a part of God's future hope for her. Even though Naomi was unaware she would suffer such losses, God knew. He planned to take her into the future, not broken, bitter, poor, or oppressed, but filled with joy and peace.

Imagine the joy this baby brought her. Her maternal instinct kicked in. I can imagine her reflecting on when she raised her other two boys. Those memories were probably bittersweet. As the baby grew, learning to crawl and walk, Naomi experienced the wonder of God's goodness in those moments.

She was there through every achievement of Obed. He probably called her name first when he began speaking. I think about how many parents wait with bated breath for a baby to say their names; I am convinced that God allowed Naomi to experience this again.

Can you envision what God was doing? God was little by little, moment by moment, healing all the wounds, hurts, and pain in her life and giving her new mercy each day. As she watched Obed grow, God was doing His transformation in her life. He was mending, molding, and rebuilding her trust and confidence in His faithfulness. God is the ultimate Parent— loving, helpful, nurturing, and giving. He does not want us to waste one day being regretful about our choices or losses. Naturally, God allows us a season to grieve, but He expects us to pick up the broken pieces of our lives and move forward. He knows we can find beauty from the ashes and joy amid sorrow because Jesus came to restore our hope and fill us with joy.

In Deuteronomy 34:8, the children of Israel grieved Moses' death for thirty days, which was the allotted time of mourning, and then God told them to move forward. This time of grieving is a perfect example of what God wants from us: grieve, get up, and move forward. He knows we are still dealing with the hurt but does not want us to stay stuck in this place of hurt and pain. God understands the pain but knows the promises and blessings in your future. You must trust Him. As Naomi trusted Him, He unfolded a new season filled with peace and love.

Let me remind you again what God did for Naomi. He rescued her from a pagan land and returned her home where she belonged. God reunited her with her people, returning her to the shelter of His protection. He restored everything Naomi had lost following the deaths of her husband and sons by orchestrating the presence of a daughter-in-law, whom He used to reinstate her standing in society.

God renewed her faith, trust, confidence, and love for Him, daily. He strengthened her and, like the eagles, caused her to soar above each stormy day and pain. He revived her by adding Obed to her life. The baby was a source of joy.

God showed her that her legacy was not lost and gave her someone to stay close to her in old age. God provided her a place within the generational line of King David by giving her a seed through Ruth. This seed, Obed, ensured the continuation of her generational line and put her in the lineage of Jesus.

God gave Naomi more than a new beginning. He gave her a legacy that has lived on for centuries through Obed's lineage. What a mighty, faithful God we serve.

In recent years, I have walked with several friends and my family through seasons of grief. To say they were all devastated is truly an understatement. One friend lost her husband after a brave battle with cancer, and another unexpectedly lost her daughter. The death of any loved one is devastating, but an unexpected death is beyond comprehension.

Getting a call that your loved one has passed can take your breath away. There are no words to describe the impact of such news. My friend who lost her daughter told me how shocking the news was and the depth and severity of her hurt and disbelief. Her grief was profound.

My friend, while her husband was dying from cancer, grieved deeply and profusely wept as she faced the possibility he would not recover.

It is painful and heartbreaking to watch those you love grieve. Even as I encouraged and prayed for these loved ones, I wept along with them. Sometimes, I reflect out loud that these people are no longer with us. I must remind myself that they are in God's presence, experiencing fullness of life and joy.

My family and friends have been broken during these painful seasons, but they have not given up. They persevere through each day because they trust God to heal their broken hearts. They have remained unstoppable in their faith and confidence in God's faithfulness.

Are you grieving today? Remember, there is hope in Jesus Christ. He will heal, help, restore, and renew you. He will be a safe place and a buffer in the pain and grief. He is with you in each stormy season. He promised never to leave you nor forsake you.

Will you rest in His faithfulness today?

Jesus can be trusted to calm the storms in your life.

Ruth's New Beginning

When we read Ruth's story, we are often transported to a place of joy and hopefulness because she was victorious over devastating heartbreaks. She reaped double for her troubles. She found a home and had a great future filled with abundance. God rescued her from poverty. She married one of the wealthiest men in her century. God showed His love and approval in her life.

Have you ever wondered what happened to her after all God provided her? Let's explore this.

As was mentioned in chapter six, she married Boaz, her kinsman-redeemer, and was lifted from poverty and out of obscurity. The marriage gave Ruth a new beginning. She was previously a widow and a stranger in a strange land. Remember, she was a Moabite. She had served pagan gods.

In chapter two, I delved into Ruth's heritage, exploring the background and societal norms that shaped her. As we look at her legacy, let's remember that after coming out of Moab, she clung to Naomi and her newfound relationship with God. She did not reflect any of the traits of her previous ancestors or the moral decay she came from. She was clothed with humility, decency, and strength.

Ruth was now living under the shelter of the one true living God, enjoying the benefits of being one of His children. She no longer had to worry about starving to death. Because of the customs of the Israelites, Ruth did not have to carry the burden of caring for Naomi alone. Boaz, her new husband, protected her from any harm she might have encountered. She had a place of honor among the women in her society. God truly blessed and elevated her. Her new beginning was beyond comprehension because God set the stage for this. Journey with me as I remind you who the Bible says Boaz's parents were.

In Matthew 16, we unravel the intriguing lineage of Boaz, tracing it back to Rahab, the courageous prostitute who aided the two Israeli spies sent by Joshua to spy out the Promised Land. The people wanted to kill them. Rahab hid them in her house, which allowed them to escape unharmed. I shared this story in my book, *Called and Chosen for Destiny*.

The Lord was gracious to Rahab and saved her and her family. She lived among the Israelites, and Salmon, one of Israel's leaders, married her. As a result of this union, Boaz was born. As I studied this, I could not help but reflect on the fact that Boaz's mother was a foreigner, just like Ruth. His mother's background made it easier for him to embrace Ruth.

Rahab was a Canaanite woman, a Gentile, and a prostitute who became a heroine of the faith. She is a testament to how God incorporated us Gentiles into His plan. Her inclusion in Boaz lineage, a blend of Gentile and Jewish heritage, vividly illustrates the divine merging of diverse backgrounds into the overarching narrative of God's redemptive work.

As previously shared, Boaz became Ruth and Naomi's kinsman-redeemer, rescuing them from destruction.

I mentioned this in an earlier chapter. *Over the years, I have heard many women say they are waiting on their Boaz. They are looking for more than wealth in the spouses they seek.* Let's look more closely at what they are seeking. Let's remember who he was and what he did.

Boaz was a man of great character. He displayed generosity not only in assisting Ruth and those employed under him but also in extending a helping hand to individuals facing poverty who gleaned in his fields. Boaz had a kind heart and served his people well.

In his interactions with Ruth and Naomi, you see a man filled with compassion as he deals with their struggles. He respected Ruth and demanded that his workers afford her the same courtesy. He charged them not to harm or do anything that would embarrass her.

Boaz acted with great integrity by protecting Ruth's reputation when he found her lying at his feet. He respected the law and customs when he gave the relative next in line the first opportunity to buy Naomi's husband's property and marry Ruth. Boaz had humility, a rare gift in many societies, especially today. His integrity seeped out as you read the story of his dealings with Ruth. He was clothed with strength and honor. He was faithful in his dealings with others. He was a man of wisdom and led with wisdom.

Many women desire these qualities in their future spouses. God blessed Ruth by providing such a spouse. This marriage gave Ruth a fresh new beginning. Ruth found rest from her labor and peace in each new day by marrying Boaz. He lifted Ruth out of a life filled with uncertainty. She had a stable home and servants who took care of her needs. Ruth received beauty for all the ashes that she had previously experienced in her life. Let's walk in her shoes for a moment.

As you read this synopsis, you, too, may long to experience this rest from all your struggles. Ruth could let go of her daily stress after God rescued her. She no longer had to do the back-breaking work of gleaning the fields. She had a safe place to rest her head at night and did not have to worry about the next day.

I am reminded of this passage in Matthew 6:25-34 as I reflect on what God did in Ruth's life. As we explore the passage, remember these promises were not just for Ruth or others in the Bible but also for you. Receive them and trust God to unfold them in your life each day.

Therefore, I tell you, do not worry about your life, what you will eat or drink, or about your body, what you will wear. Is not life more than food, and the body more than clothes? Look at the birds of the air; they do not sow or reap or store away in barns, and yet your heavenly Father feeds them. Are you not much more valuable than they? Can any one of you, by worrying, add a single hour to your life? "And why do you worry about clothes? See how the flowers of the field grow. They do not labor or spin. Yet I tell you that not even Solomon, in all his splendor, was dressed like one of these. If that is how God clothes the grass of the field, which is here today and tomorrow is thrown into the fire, will he not much more clothe you—you of little faith? So do not worry, saying, 'What shall we eat?' or 'What shall we drink?' or 'What shall we wear?' For the pagans run after all these things, and your heavenly Father knows that you need them. But seek first his kingdom and his righteousness, and all these things will be given to you as well. Therefore, do not worry about tomorrow, for tomorrow will worry about itself. Each day has enough trouble of its own.

Matthew 6:25-34 (NIV)

Ruth experienced the promises of this scripture. Like Ruth, we need to embrace these promises. God will honor His promises in your life. We are encouraged not to worry about our lives, what we eat or drink, and what we wear. Let's dissect what the scripture is telling us. It says the birds of the air do not sow or reap because God takes care of them.

Let's look at the history of birds to understand why this scripture is so powerful. The *CK-12 Foundation* says birds are essential to humans because they provide food and fertilizer. They are critical to the ecosystems because they are essential pollinators. When thinking of all the animals in the world, birds are said to be some of the most intelligent creatures. There are over ten thousand species in the world.

Jesus tells us birds do not sow, reap, or store food away in barns, but our heavenly Father feeds them. Jesus asks, "Are you not more valuable than they?" This is an important question for many who worry about not having enough to handle their daily needs. Many people around the world need more finances to buy food to eat. We have witnessed this struggle as we have ministered and served in the United States and worldwide.

A short while ago, I saw a homeless woman getting food from a trash can. I approached her and asked about her life and what led her to this heartbreaking place. With many tears and lots of regret, she told me her story.

This woman had no finances to meet her needs. In this scripture passage, Jesus addresses her and many like her who find themselves in similar situations. God wants us to know He feeds all the birds on the earth. Not one of the birds He created goes without a meal. The birds expect to be fed. They do not ask how or by whom. They look for food at mealtime, which is always available because God provides it. Jesus invites you to trust that, much like his care for the birds, despite their lesser value, He is committed to meeting all your needs. This assurance is rooted in the fact that you belong to Him, and your life holds immense value in His eyes.

For some people, completely trusting God is a hard thing to do. I am raising my hands. I am in a season I call "Walking on water faith," as I believe God will provide for the next level in our ministries. One day, the Lord told me to be like the three Hebrew boys and get in the fire. Again, He said Daniel went into the lion's den even though his life was in jeopardy.

The challenge He issued me is this: Your life is not in peril, and partial obedience is not obedience. Your faith must go to another level to attain the fullness of your destiny. You must trust me more. I need to trust Him like the birds trust Him to feed them.

Is He challenging you in any way? Like the birds, you *must believe* and trust Him. Ask yourself, "Do I genuinely believe I am more valuable to God than birds?

We are then told in the scripture not to worry about clothes because God has clothed the flowers of the field in more splendor than Solomon. As king, Solomon was dressed in expensive, beautiful, and elaborate garments, yet God says his clothing could not compare with the flowers of the field.

For just a moment, think about the flowers you have seen throughout your lifetime. Beautiful, right? Their colors are a marvel to behold. We love flowers for their fragrances, textures, shapes, and, naturally, their colors. The pattern on the flowers guides bees, butterflies, and other pollinators to the nectar. God tells us that Solomon's regal clothes cannot be compared to the beauty of the flowers we see daily.

Since the flowers do not labor to become who they are, we should not struggle to trust God to meet our needs. God created the flowers and 'clothed' the grass in the field. He will clothe you. The flowers and the grass are here one day and gone the next, so God asks, "*Will he not much more clothe you.*"

He tells us our faith is small because we do not trust Him
to do this fundamental thing—clothe us.

You are told not to worry about your food, drink, and

clothes because your heavenly Father knows you need them. Since He knows this, He will provide for it. Ruth discovered this when she encountered God. He freed her from worry, and she could enjoy God's gifts without stressing how she and Naomi would survive.

The scripture says the pagans run after food, clothes, and daily needs. They do this because they do not have a loving Father, God, who provides for them. We are God's children and can rest in His faithfulness and promises for our lives. God will provide these things to us as we seek His kingdom daily. We are reminded that tomorrow, we will have many more worries and troubles we must face and overcome. We do not have to focus on tomorrow. It will take care of itself. Ruth was living out these promises.

A few years ago, I had regular headaches. Someone told me this was because I was living in the future and worrying about tomorrow. I remember God gives us fresh grace each day. I was attempting to live on the next day's grace, and I needed to let tomorrow take care of itself. I received these wise words and began living each day as I should, and the headaches diminished. Today, I seldom get headaches because each time I worry about tomorrow, I remind myself of this. I still struggle with focusing on today and not worrying about tomorrow, so I keep at it until I prevail.

Ruth trusted God because she learned He honors His word. Shortly after Ruth married Boaz, she gave birth to her first child, Obed. The Bible records in 1 Chronicles 2:12 that Obed was the father of Jesse.

It's important to note this scripture is the only recorded act of Obed's life. We can ask, is this all he did? If this was his only accomplishment, it was a hugely significant one.

Boaz and Ruth lived in Bethlehem, Obed's birthplace. As previously mentioned, Obed was the grandfather of King David, who was born in Bethlehem. Bethlehem is also the birthplace of Jesus, our Savior. Can you see how God aligned all these events?

Even though Naomi's family left the place of God's provision and protection, the family lineage was not severed. God is infinite in His mercy and knows how to redeem our lives even when we make bad decisions. Through Ruth and Naomi's lineage, God birthed His greatest gift, JESUS, into the world.

The Bible does not record whether or not Ruth had additional children. The last mention of her was in Ruth chapter 4 after giving birth to Obed. It's interesting to note that the book of Ruth ends with Naomi being the one praised by the women. They declared that God did not leave Naomi without a kinsman-redeemer. They prayed that God would make him famous throughout Israel and sustain her in old age. They prophesied over Naomi and blessed her instead of Ruth.

What about Ruth? Was this not her story, her son? Yes. The women gave Ruth credit for loving Naomi and being better to her than ten sons but did not mention she was Obed's mother. Why? This story was about the lineage of Elimelek, Naomi's husband, and ultimately the birth of Jesus Christ through their ancestry.

As I mentioned previously, the book of Ruth was primarily about Naomi from beginning to end. She was God's primary focus. Ruth was blessed because of her association with Naomi. Being aligned with the right people can catapult you into your destiny and position you to receive the blessings God wants to pour into your life. These alignments are God's divine appointments for you. You must consistently seek God so He can order your steps to the right places and people.

Let's ask the question: What happened to Boaz and Ruth after the birth of Obed? Keep reading as I share what some historians and Jewish scholars have to say about their lives after Obed's birth.

Remember, I previously told you Boaz was approximately eighty years old and Ruth forty when they married? Well, there are no records of what happened to Ruth following this. However, some Jewish scholars, the Jewish Women's Archive, the Encyclopedia of Jewish Women, some historians, and other encyclopedias tell us that Boaz died shortly after marrying Ruth. Some even say he died the next day, and this is the reason why Naomi was the one who raised his son, Obed. Throughout my research, the result was the same—Boaz died right after marrying Ruth. Let me ask the question some of you may be pondering. If Boaz indeed died right after marriage, why would God allow Ruth to marry a man of such great character and then let him die so soon?

This story was about something other than
Boaz and Ruth.

It was always about the true Kinsman-Redeemer, Jesus. He is the only one who can provide lasting change. He is the only one that can redeem us for all eternity. Jesus is the only one who can truly save us. He is the only one who helps us advance into the better future, He has planned for us. Only Jesus can guide and direct our steps. He makes our futures safe, secure, and bright.

I repeat it, JESUS IS THE ONLY ONE WE CANNOT LIVE WITHOUT.

It is hard to reflect that Ruth was possibly a widow in such a short time and had to begin all over again. However, let's remember that she was not in the same situation. She had risen above the hardships of her previous life. No longer poor. Not a foreigner without prospects. No longer an outcast.

Ruth was set up for life because Boaz's wealth was passed on to her and her son. She had a support system that she did not previously have. She had the gift of a son who had to be raised and trained. God had selected her for this excellent task and provided Naomi to help raise her son. God marked them both for greatness. The women of Naomi's generation prophesied that God had a plan. God did not leave Ruth comfortless.

Ruth's son, Obed, married and made Ruth a grandmother. She wasn't alone now; she had family. Although Obed only had one son, Jesse had five sons, including David.

Imagine this—Ruth was King David's great-grandmother. Jesse was Ruth's grandson, so his sons were Ruth's grandchildren. David, who had nineteen children, extended Ruth's family line, resulting in numerous great-grandchildren and a substantial legacy. One of David's sons, Solomon, became the next king after his death. What a tremendous legacy God gave Ruth. She was a significant part of the lineage of Jesus Christ.

God used this Moabite woman to fulfill a significant purpose on earth. God was her constant companion, Ruth's helper, and her true kinsman-redeemer. God was better to her than Boaz could ever be. He gave her life, a place in history, and a legacy that outlived her. This legacy continues today because of what one of her ancestors, Jesus Christ, accomplished at Calvary—our redemption. We are a part of this lineage because the Bible says we are heirs and joint heirs with Jesus.

For the many women asking for their Boaz, remember that although Boaz was a man of outstanding character, he was no replacement for God in Ruth's life. Your Boaz will not be a replacement for Jesus, your Kinsman-Redeemer. No one can ever take the place of the Godhead (Father, Son, and Holy Spirit) in your life. I repeat: *the only person we cannot live without is Jesus.* So, as you pray for your Boaz, remember to seek after Jesus more and trust that He knows the best plan for your life. God is the giver of the greatest gift you can ever receive— the love of His beloved Son, Jesus, and His sacrificial death on the cross of Calvary for you.

After His resurrection, Jesus sent you a powerful Helper, the Holy Spirit, to live in you and be with you throughout your life (John 14:16-17). You are deeply loved.

If marriage is your desire, take heart and continue to believe your Boaz exists. He will find you when you love and seek after Jesus, the great lover of your soul, with all your heart. Jesus will lead you to the one He chose for you before the foundation of the world.

Do not fear that your Boaz will die shortly after marriage because God is with you, and no two stories are alike. Our journeys to our destinies are different, but Jesus knows the way. He will lead you down the right path, just as God led Ruth down the right path to an outstanding future.

Let me repeat it: Ruth, the foreigner, was King David's great-grandmother, which placed her in the lineage of Jesus Christ, God's Son. If God did this for Ruth, He most assuredly will do phenomenal things in your life. He made Ruth unstoppable and will do the same with you.

CHAPTER 10

Jesus, Our Victory

Throughout this book, I have shared Ruth and Naomi's journey, struggles, and victories, along with others who faced great hardships and struggles. These people persevered. They were unstoppable as they pursued better futures for themselves and their loved ones. Here is a recap:

- The death of Naomi's husband and children.
- The death of Ruth's husband and her refusal to leave Naomi's side.
- Ruth and Naomi were poor and struggled to meet their daily needs.
- Ruth did back-breaking work as a gleaner in Boaz's field to feed her and Naomi.
- We examined the hardness of their journey and some of our journeys.

- We tackled the subject of weariness as we battled hard times.
- We examined God's divine connection in the marriage of Boaz and Ruth.
- The birth of Obed, who was Ruth and Boaz's son. Obed added purpose to Naomi's life.
- We learned about the relationship of the kinsman-redeemer who helped family members during hard times, restoring their lives and fortunes.
- Boaz was a relative of Naomi's husband and the kinsman-redeemer God used to restore her life and fortunes.
- We learned Boaz was only a shadow *(reflection)* of our true Kinsman-Redeemer, Jesus.
- We discovered that God grants us new beginnings.
- We learned that when facing brokenness, we can still be unstoppable by asking God for help.

I have had many seasons of new beginnings. Sometimes, these seasons were after significant losses—jobs, health, finances, deaths of loved ones, etc. Some of you have also had new beginnings due to substantial losses. We mourn many things in life. Once we complete the grieving process, most people will begin a new journey. However, I have met a few people who did not choose to embrace a new life and a fresh start over the years.

The tragedies in their lives were too insurmountable, and they remained stuck in their situations. Following the death of her husband, one lady never recovered and developed mental challenges that affected the rest of her life. God offers each of us new beginnings. I often say, "If you are still here, God is not done with you yet. He still has a great plan for your future."

I encourage you to embrace the great future God has for you and enjoy the new beginning He desires to give you. Journey with me as we look at Jesus' new beginnings.

Have you ever considered that Jesus had two new beginnings? Yes, He did. As previously shared, Jesus has always existed with God. He was in the beginning with God and said yes to His earthly assignment of redeeming humanity.

Let's think about this again. Jesus lived with God in Heaven, yet came to Earth and lived in one of His female creations, Mary, for nine months. God became a baby in the form of His Son, Jesus, and started a new life on Earth. He had a new beginning. Jesus grew from a baby to a toddler, then a youth, a teenager, a young adult, and ultimately into adulthood when He began fulfilling His destiny at thirty years old.

He started over. He started from scratch, just as we did.

As I wrote the above statement, I could not help but be amazed at what Jesus did. I marvel that He was willing to surrender His position and status to walk in our shoes from birth to adulthood. Jesus undertook this journey to intimately connect with our challenges and triumphs, to secure our redemption, and to share these experiences with His Father, God, as He intercedes for us each day.

Approximately one thousand years after Ruth and Naomi's existence, Jesus identified with their new beginnings because of His death on the cross. In this new beginning, Jesus gave everything and willingly died a horrible death so that one day, you would be free to fulfill your destiny in Him.

The Bible tells us that once He accomplished His purpose on Earth—redeeming humankind—He ascended into heaven. Acts 1:11 records this: *"Men of Galilee," they said, "Why do you stand here looking into the sky? This same Jesus, who has been taken from you into heaven, will come back in the same way you have seen him go into heaven."*

After His death on the cross, Jesus went home. He went back to His Father in heaven. Jesus was acknowledged as the Son of God and the world's Savior, thanks to His transformative sacrifice on the cross. Before dying, He had a high-level status in heaven as God's Son. As our Savior, our *Kinsman-Redeemer*, His new status, and new beginning are described in Philippians 4:9-11. Come with me as we explore this scripture and gain insight into His tremendous sacrifice and great reward.

Wherefore God also hath highly exalted him, and given him a name which is above every name: that at the name of Jesus every knee should bow, of things in heaven, and things in Earth, and things under the Earth; and that every tongue should confess that Jesus Christ is Lord, to the glory of God the Father.
Philippians 2:9-11 (KJV)

These verses are known as the exaltations of Jesus Christ. Exaltation is most often used when talking about God and Jesus. It was also used when talking about Israel and its Kings. The word means to lift up.

In the Old Testament, we see that God alone could be exalted. His power is far beyond any others. He was especially exalted because of His mighty acts—the parting of the Red Sea, the manna from heaven, and providing water out of the rock, etc. (Isaiah 2:11, Job 36:22, Psalm 46:10). In the same way, Jesus was exalted after the cross. He was highly exalted for His accomplishments. The journey to His exaltation required humbling Himself and dying on a lowly Roman cross.

Jesus took several steps from the cross back to the throne of God. Let's review them in the scripture:

Step 1: God has highly exalted Him.
Step 2: Given Him a name that is above every other name.
Step 3: In the name of Jesus, every knee will bow.
Step 4: Every tongue will confess.
Step 5: Jesus is Lord to the glory of God the Father.

God Highly Exalted Him

God highly exalted Jesus. He gave Him the highest place of honor because He sacrificed His life. God gave Jesus the highest rank/status in heaven. He was exalted over every other being in heaven, second only to God in power and position. God elevated Jesus to a position of power and authority at His right hand.

It is safe to say God did this because His Son was obedient and chose suffering and a horrific death to redeem humankind and reunite us with His Father, God. What joy it is to report that Jesus chose suffering so that we could have a relationship with Him. God wanted you to be a part of His family, so He gave His ALL to accomplish this.

When God created Adam, God was very involved in Adam's life. He was not distant but was present with him each day. He met Adam daily, talked, and helped him name all the animals. *God was a loving parent who groomed His son, Adam, for success. It is evident God created a family with Adam and then with Eve. You are a part of the family of God, and He wants you to be successful.* He will walk and talk with you daily to ensure your success and victory. Invite Him to reveal how welcome you are as a part of His family.

Romans 8:17 says, "Now if we are children, then we are heirs —of God and co-heirs with Christ if indeed we share in his suffer- ings so that we may also share in his glory." The scripture says that as children, you are heirs and co-heirs to Jesus. Being heirs and co-heirs means all that Jesus owns you own. God has granted you the same rights and privileges as His beloved Son, Jesus. You are special to Him, and you belong to His family.

Please give me some creative license here. The first Adam was disobedient and lost his and, subsequently, our authority in the Garden of Eden. He and Eve relinquished theirs and our positions as sons and daughters with our heavenly Father to the devil. This act is why Jesus, who is known as the second Adam, had to come and die.

Can you imagine what was taking place in heaven as the Father and the heavenly hosts watched Jesus enter the Garden of Gethsemane to pray and prepare Himself for His death on the cross?

As He prayed for strength and then surrendered to God's will, I imagine a cheer went up in heaven. JESUS SAID YES! As the earthly authorities accused him, He still said YES! As Jesus was beaten, He said YES! As He struggled to carry the cross, He said YES. As they drove the nails into His broken body, He said YES! As He hung on the cross in agonizing pain, all heaven knew what God had always known—His obedient Son, Jesus, would always say YES to His will.

This tremendous sacrifice is the reason God has highly exalted Jesus! He is and has always been an OBEDIENT SON.

Given Him A Name That Is Above Every Other Name

Matthew 1:23 gives us the name above every other name—Immanuel, which means "God with us."

Many children during Jesus' century had the name Jesus, but in Luke 1:26-38, we see the name Son of the Most High God. Jesus is known as Savior, Redeemer, Only Begotten Son of God, Beloved Son, the Bread of Life, the Lord, etc. Jesus earned the name Son of the Most-High God because of His victory on the cross.

Without the shedding of His blood, we would still be

captured by sin; we would have no relationship with God, our Father, and we would be living in the depths of despair. Many of us would be destroyed by the vicious attacks of the devil. Because of Jesus' sacrifice, we have the power to overcome. We can boldly declare, *"Greater is He that is in me than He that is in the world (1 John 4:4)."*

At The Name Of Jesus, Every Knee Will Bow

When Jesus came to Earth for the first time, He was in the form of a baby. When He comes again, He will be the reigning King of heaven. Jesus will be in His former glory as our mighty Redeemer. He will be our conquering King.

Every knee will bow to Jesus.

The word *every* means every. Not one knee will not bow to the mighty name of Jesus. Every earthly King and leader will bow. Every creature and every person will bow. No one will be left standing. It is not a question of whether they *will* bow. They will have *no choice* but to bow because the government of heaven will command them to bow.

The devil and all his demons will have to bow.

Bow means to bend the head or body in total submission. It is to show respect. The devil, demons, and unbelievers will bow low in the presence of King Jesus. Everyone on the Earth will bow in acknowledgment of God's ultimate authority. Bowing expresses honor, respect, worship, and humility/humiliation.

The question we must ask ourselves is, will people bow of their own free will because they have said YES to Jesus Christ and are a part of the family of God, or will they be compelled to bow because they rejected Him and belong to the devil's kingdom? I pray you will freely bow your knees because you love and serve the one and only Son of God, Jesus.

Every Tongue Will Confess Jesus is Lord

When the scripture says 'every tongue,' it means all people in every nation and language. Every creature who has a tongue will also confess Jesus is Lord. *Confess* means acknowledging and admitting that Jesus is who He has always said He was— Savior and Messiah. It also means declaring what is fact—Jesus alone is Lord. Since every tongue will confess, this tells us there will be a lot of loud yelling. People will vocally, loudly, and publicly acknowledge and publicly declare the Lordship of Jesus Christ. Heaven, Earth, and hell will thunderously make this declaration. Eventually, every person will declare Jesus is Lord. No one will be exempt from making this declaration. They will have no choice but to proclaim what is FACT—Jesus

Christ, the Son of God, our Redeemer, and our Savior ALONE is Lord.

Those who have previously accepted this as fact will enjoy a profound time in history with the Son of God. Those who refuse to acknowledge Jesus will have to make this confession because they will have no choice. When they stand before the Great White Throne Judgment, they will be judged and separated from Jesus throughout eternity. They will join the devil and his demons in the lake of fire.

The devil and his demons will bow low and acknowledge JESUS CHRIST IS LORD. The devil will be exposed as the liar and fraud he is after thousands of years of destroying lives. The problem is that many people who believe the devil will find out too late that they followed the wrong leader. They will spend eternity forever separated from Jesus.

The coming of Jesus and the rapture of Believers will be a joyous celebration for those who accepted Jesus as their personal Savior and Lord. All these confessions of Jesus will be for the glory of only ONE—GOD. Jesus Christ is Lord to the glory of God the Father.

All notably, Believers in Jesus Christ will all have new beginnings. Naomi, Ruth, Boaz, and Jesus experienced new beginnings. Think about the many times you have started over. Jesus, your Redeemer, allowed you to make different choices. If you have made wrong choices/decisions, you can start again. It is not too late.

Naomi, having followed her husband to Moab and subsequently endured the loss of him, her children, and all earthly possessions, found a new lease on life and embarked on a fresh start. The birth of Obed gave her a new life. She had an opportunity to pour her love into this baby. She could care for him when he needed the most love and care. As she watched for, nursed, and taught him, this became her lifeline—the reason she was still alive. She thought her life was over, but God gave her a new beginning. Please note that she could have chosen to stay in the bitterness invading her soul, but she said YES to God. Saying yes caused her to step out of the shadows of her life and into a new beginning, a new season, a fresh start.

Ruth embraced her new beginning. She did not hesitate to take a giant step forward into the future. Her new beginning was different from Naomi's. She had to be open to accepting a new husband and becoming another man's wife. This marriage meant adapting to a new person and environment, but she said YES to a new tomorrow. Her new beginning, her fresh start, led her into unfamiliar territories. Still, she embraced the newness and surrendered her plans to provide a home, safety, and provision for herself and Naomi. Ruth embraced her new beginning while trusting God to walk her through each difficult day ahead. He did, and she prospered. We are still hearing about her today. She left a great legacy in the Earth.

A Child's New Beginning

I was ministering and conducting missions in Zimbabwe, Africa, a few years ago. As is our custom, we found one of the poorest hospitals to visit. We met a young girl, who was ten years old, in a hospital. She was in the hospital due to a bad car accident that left her with severe burns over 40% of her body;

her mother had died in the accident. When we initially met her, she appeared healthy and robust. The Holy Spirit prompted me to ask why she was in the hospital since she seemed healthy. The nurse said that she had been in the hospital for over a year because her father was unable to pay the medical bills, which they estimated to be almost $5,000. The hospital would not release her until the father paid the medical bill.

After my initial shocked reaction, I was again prompted by the Holy Spirit to gather more information about her. Before leaving the hospital, the Holy Spirit told me to "Get her home for Christmas." After returning to the USA, we did a fundraising campaign. We raised the funds that got her home for Christmas and enough to pay for one year of school, all of her school clothes, counseling, and to give her dad finances to help them with a new beginning.

When the hospital called her dad to pick her up, he was fearful of them arresting him for child abandonment and felt they were trying to trap him. He refused to get her because he could not believe the story that someone paid her hospital bill. Our organizer in the county had to call him and convince him that the ministry had paid the bill in full and that God was giving them a new start.

He arrived at the hospital to retrieve her in complete amazement. God's faithfulness to them completely undid him. He could not understand how God had heard his prayers and sent people to provide the help he needed.

To say the hospital was amazed is an understatement. They printed the story in their newspaper, reaching the ears of the country's President. God was glorified because He provided for this young girl and her family. The hospital shared the news far and wide, and people knew God was still faithful to help them as they earnestly prayed.

This story reminds us that God shows us fresh mercy each day. He rescues the broken-hearted, binds up the wounds of the hurting, and sets captives free. He is a God of new beginnings. He will give you a fresh start, a do-over. Will you ask Him to do this for you today?

This young girl and her family experienced a new beginning. God, in His great mercy and compassion, reached into their lives and brought hope, healing, and restoration. He gave them a new life. He saw all they had been through and was moved with compassion to help them.

Jesus is filled with compassion for the lost and the hurting. Let's consider there were many lost, hurting, and hungry people during our trip to Zimbabwe, yet He sent us to this hospital, to this particular child and family, to bring hope and deliverance. Jesus cares about every person, but in this instance, this young girl needed immediate attention and had to be reunited with her family, so God provided the resources. Jesus is the only One who could have restored her, and He used us as His vessels. All credit and glory go to Jesus alone.

I remember the story in 1 Kings 17:7-16 when God sent Elijah to rescue a widow in Zarephath, where the land was in a famine. She and her son would have died of starvation without His intervention. When she gave Elijah her last meal, God kept her barrel overflowing with food until the famine ended.

Jesus, in Luke 4:25-26, tells us that there were many widows in Israel in the time of Elijah, yet Elijah was not sent to any of them. Instead, he was sent to the widow of Zarephath. He further says there were many lepers in Israel during Elisha the prophet's time, yet not one was cleansed—only Naaman the Syrian.

Jesus shared these two stories to remind us we are not alone. He sees and knows our struggles. Jesus is telling us He is not only mindful of those who are His elect group of people, the Israelites, but He watches over all His creation and is moved with compassion for everyone.

In highlighting these stories, Jesus reminds us that His eyes are on us. He wants us to have a fresh start. He offers us new beginnings. Since you are still alive, it is not over for you. You can begin again. You can step into a new season, receive forgiveness, release your burdens, accept His help, and receive the blessings He has for you. As long as you are alive, you have the opportunity to CHANGE. Jesus offers you the gift of freedom that is found in Him. John 8:36 says, *"So if the Son sets you free, you will be free indeed."*

Jesus cares for you. His hands are outstretched to you right now. He offers you a new beginning. Accept this wondrous gift today, and begin to run your race with perseverance, knowing you have already gained the victory. Jesus has gone ahead of you, fought the battles on your behalf, and showed you the way to victory. You CAN and MUST begin again. If you are experiencing brokenness, you have all you need to overcome and become unstoppable because Jesus is with you, cheering you on to victory.

I began this book with a question: *"Why Me?"* As you journeyed through it, have you reflected on your journey and the challenges you have faced? What have you discovered about yourself? I have asked myself that question many times. Many would say don't ask the 'why me' question but instead turn it around and say *why not me?'*

It is natural and reasonable that, at times, we may ask the 'why me' question because the struggles and pain in our lives can push us to the brink. I have asked this question amid health struggles, family struggles, financial struggles, and the daily struggles of running two ministries. These questions do not mean God is not with us. I am fully aware that He hears every prayer and sees every tear.

He helped the people in the Bible who struggled amid hardships. As you read the Psalms, David battled depression because his life was filled with challenges and difficulties. He cried out to God often for help and relief from his struggles. His pain was real and heartbreaking, and God heard and responded to his cries.

I know some people who, in their painful struggles, will ask the 'why me' question as their pain becomes unbearable. Sometimes, this question is in the form of a whimper as they battle to overcome it. I am thinking of one person in particular who experienced the horrendous pain associated with having cancer. The whimper was a heartfelt cry for quick healing or a release from their enduring pain. God heard and responded to their cry.

God understands why some of us ask the 'why me' question. He hears the groans and whimpers. He feels your pain. Remember, Jesus is touched with the feelings of your infirmities. He knows intense pain. He does not judge you for asking the 'why me' question. He will help you to see that others are also struggling and are asking the 'why me' question.

It is essential to know this because as you look at others whose struggles may be as great or even more significant than yours, you may come to the 'why *not* me' question. Jesus was not exempt from struggles and told us we would face our struggles. As a result of His sacrifice on Calvary, He has provided us victory during the pain.

Life can be filled with pain, hurt, and struggles. As we face them, we have an advocate with our Father in Heaven (1 John 2:1). The Bible tells us Jesus is seated at the right hand of God the Father. Romans 8:34 tells us that He is interceding for us. Hebrews 7:25 says Jesus lives to intercede for us.

Let's ask the question: Why would Jesus be interceding for us? The word intercede means. Jesus is praying to God on your behalf. He is intervening between God and you and pointing out to God that He understands your difficulties.

Jesus reminds His Father He has walked in your shoes and understands your pain. When God hears this from His Son, He extends you abundant grace and mercy even though you may deserve death and destruction. Jesus, seated at the right hand of God, a place of great authority, looks at you each day as you face your hardships, and I can imagine His words would go something like this—"God, I understand their pain, hurt, hardships, struggles, and brokenness." God, an eyewitness to His Son's suffering and death, hears Jesus' prayers for you, relents, and extends mercy to us.

- **You have an advocate with the Father.**
- **You are beloved.**
- **You are forgiven.**
- **You are accepted and cared for.**

Just as God loved, accepted, helped, and provided for Naomi and Ruth, He will do the same for you. He will give you an amazing future—one more extraordinary than anything you can imagine. When you feel that life has worn you down, God reminds you He is not yet finished with His plans for you.

He was not finished with Naomi and gave her a new life. He was not finished with Ruth and gave her a new beginning. He is not finished with you yet; more extraordinary days await you. Be still and know that He is God (Psalm 46:12). He is with you and will never leave your story unfinished or your life unfulfilled. He will finish the great work He so faithfully started in you. You can TRUST His Word.

As we studied and reflected on Naomi and Ruth's journey and their legacy, let me ask these questions, "How is your journey going?" "What will your legacy be?"

Remember, you get to write your life script. God will direct your every step and get you to the desired destination. Stay the course. Keep pressing forward. The only way to fail and miss His great plans for your future is to give up when the pain is unbearable. Although broken, you can still be an unstoppable force on Earth.

———

Jesus will heal and restore you. You can begin again.

———

A Prayer for Healing Over Brokenness!

Lord, there are times when my heart feels bruised and broken. The pain seems unending. In those times when I cry out to You, I know You alone have the answer for my brokenness. I am never alone, for You are with me.

Father, I am often reminded of Jesus' broken body and the many stripes He took on His back to secure my healing and freedom. Jesus, I appropriate your bruises for my healing. I thank you for your sacrifice.

Father, *Isaiah 43:2* tells me when I pass through the waters, You will be with me; and when I pass through the rivers, they will not sweep over me. When I walk through the fire, I will not be burned; the flames will not set me ablaze.

Psalm 46:1 says you are my refuge and strength, an ever-present help in trouble. I am genuinely grateful You are my shelter in the storms. You are always with me when trouble comes my way.

Father, *Psalm 147:3* says You heal the brokenhearted and bind their wounds. This verse describes me. Therefore, I receive this promise. You steady me when my heart is breaking. Oh, how you comfort me and fill me with strength.

John 16:33 says You have told me these things, so that in You I may have peace. In this world, I will have trouble. But take heart: You have overcome the world. It is apparent throughout the scriptures that one of Your great desires for me is to be at peace. Help me to anchor myself daily in Your peace. I take comfort in *2 Corinthians 12:9*, But he said to me, "My grace is sufficient for you, for my power is made perfect in weakness." Therefore, I will boast all the more gladly about my weaknesses so that Christ's power may rest on me. You are my all-sufficiency.

I am forever grateful for what *Philippians 4:19* tells me. You will meet all my needs according to the riches of Your glory in Christ Jesus. Father, all my needs include emotional, spiritual, relational, and financial, as well as healing and restoration. You promise You will care for each one, in Jesus' name.

Jesus, when fear attempts to overtake me, I am reminded of when You walked the earth and how You bravely faced and overcame fear in the garden of Gethsemane. Your bravery is my example of conquering fear. Because You knew fear was the greatest weapon the devil would use against me, You have provided scriptures to combat it. *Isaiah 41:10* says so do not fear, for I am with you; do not be dismayed, for I am your God. I will strengthen you and help you; I will uphold you with my righteous right hand.

Father, I have been broken many times, but you have armed me with strength and made me unstoppable in the fiery trials sent against me. Jesus, with You, I am always victorious. Jesus, with You, I will conquer every enemy. Jesus, by your stripes, I am healed.

I am and will always be unstoppable because you are with me.

AMEN!

I am unstoppable! Therefore, I Win!

A Prayer for Salvation

Father, I acknowledge You sent Jesus into the world to die for my sins. I believe He is Your Son, who was born of a virgin, and He died and rose from the dead for my sins. I acknowledge I have sinned and fallen short of Your standards, and I ask You to forgive me.

I invite Jesus to come into my heart because the Bible says He is the way, truth, and life, and no man comes to the Father but by Him. Father, I am coming to You in the precious name of Your Son, Jesus. I thank You for saving me and setting me free, in Jesus' name.

Amen - So Be It.

Notes

Chapters 1-10
Zondervan Bible Commentary
FF Bruce, General Edition
(Grand Rapids, MI)

Chapters 1-10
Vine's Expository Dictionary
Edited by Stephen D. Renn
Hendrickson Publishers Marketing LLC

Chapters 1-10
All the Books and Chapters of the Bible
1972, Zondervan Publishing House
Grand Rapids, MI

Chapters 1-10
The Illustrated Dictionary & Concordance of the Bible
General Editor, Geoffrey Wigoder, PH.D.

Sterling Publishing Co. Inc., New York

Chapters 1-10

Dictionary-Merriam-Webster.com Thesaurus, Merriam-Webster.

https://www.merriam-webster.com/thesaurus/dictionary

You Can TRUST Him

      Have you ever faced what seemed like an impossible task? As you looked at what you needed to accomplish, you felt like giving up even before you started. There are seasons in life when we face things that wear us down. These things are designed to stop us from persevering to our victorious end. At times, we have exerted all our strength and are worn out by the effort to accomplish these tasks. In the midst of the struggles, we can get discouraged and may want to quit. Sometimes we feel there is no point in continuing, and if we do decide to continue, we may choose only to put forth the minimum effort. At other times, we may pray for God's help to overcome these obstacles, so we can get better results. During these times you will find God is available to help you. You will also discover what may be impossible for you is definitely possible with Him.

      When God gives you an assignment, He fully understands you will need Him in order to successfully accomplish it. He wants to be intricately involved with you in its fulfillment. Ask yourself, "Am I fulfilling my part or attempting to do His part?" Remember, there are things only God can do, and the things He assigns to you, you are capable of handling with His help. Hebrews 10:35-38 says, *"So do not throw away your confidence; it will be richly rewarded. You need to persevere so that when you have done the will of God, you will receive what he has promised."*

As you are persevering, you must hold on to your confidence in God. Your journey is not in vain, there is a reward at the end for a job well done. You will receive His promises for your life. Why does God require us to persevere? Because it is developing attitudes in our lives—character, faithfulness, strength, and tenacity. These will help us reach a victorious end and cause us to receive all the promises that are assigned to our lives.

Perseverance helps us get stronger: stronger in our thoughts, emotions, character, and physical makeup. Through perseverance, we grow and become better than we were. When God gives us an assignment, He equips us to complete it. If He allows a situation that is causing you to have to press harder towards its accomplishment, then He knows this will produce good fruit in your life. The enemy cannot bring anything into your life that God does not know about. If God allows it to come to you, He knows the fruit this will birth in and through you to impact others for Him.

Galatians 6:9 says, *"Let us not become weary in doing good, for at the proper time we will reap a harvest if we do not give up."*

The scripture acknowledges we are prone to get weary as we persevere. It encourages us to not allow weariness to set in and overtake us. It's important to note it says we can get weary even while doing good, meaning things that benefit others; things that advance the kingdom of God; and things that are helping those struggling in life. As I type these statements, I think of the many people who are caretakers to elderly parents and struggle under the immense workload. I also think about those who have had to deal with family members who are enduring severe sicknesses. In these shocking situations, Jesus tells us not to get weary while doing these good things.

How is it possible to keep weariness at bay? By seeking His help at all times, by allowing Him to work alongside and in you; by casting your cares on Him moment by moment because the Bible tells us He cares about us. He wants to yoke up with you, so He can help you to carry your heavy load (Matthew 11:30).

I am reminded of an elderly lady I met in a grocery store a few years ago. I had left my grocery basket for a moment and when I returned to it, she was holding on to it and would not let go. She thought this was her basket and we were shopping together. When I realized she suffered from Alzheimer's, I tried to locate the people to whom she belonged. I couldn't help wondering to myself how they had allowed her to wander off without supervision. She began to follow me throughout the store as I attempted to find a store employee to make an announcement for her family. Then she started touching people and a few of them reacted with irritation before I had a chance to explain she was having some health struggles.

Finally, an elderly man came looking for her. He was extremely irritated she had wandered off and he yelled at her, grabbed her hand, and pulled her away. This was a man who was struggling with weariness while doing good. A few minutes later as I went into another aisle, there she was again by herself playing with a teenager's hair. The mother of the teenager simply did not know what to do. I stopped and explained her struggles, and someone would come and get her. The elderly gentleman showed up again, still overcome with irritation. Let's walk in his shoes for a moment. He was having to take care of her (possibly his wife), while she was oblivious to what was going on around her. He was persevering through difficult times and his weariness was evident.

Jesus wants to help you with weariness. He says if you do not give up, then at the right time you will receive a harvest. Our challenge is we do not know when the right time is, so we have to persevere until we get to it and receive the reward. This requires help that only Jesus can give us. Listen: God only ever asks us to do our part. He never asks us to do what He alone can do. As you do your part, persevering, He will give you the breakthroughs. Perseverance is not easy but it is necessary.

Perseverance Is A Must

Have you ever had to persevere through hard, difficult times? I believe perseverance is the key that unlocks the doors in our lives and gives us entrance into God's blessings. If you give up when the way is paved with difficulties, you will miss the greatest opportunities to know God and His Son in a rich and fulfilling way. Perseverance means to abide, be steady, endure, to be patient, to persist, and to not give up.

1 Corinthians 15:58 says, "*Therefore, my dear brothers, stand firm. Let nothing move you. Always give yourselves fully to the work of the Lord, because you know that your labor is not in vain in Him.*" The scripture tells you to

be steady, let nothing move you, stay on course because you are not laboring for anything.

In a race, the person who persists and never gives up in the face of adversity will always triumph. I saw this clearly while ministering in Guatemala. If you have never been to Guatemala, one of the things you should know is it is very mountainous. As we traveled from city to city, I prayed intensely as the van struggled up these mountains that were so steep, that I feared we would tip over. During one of these trips, I saw a lady carrying a stack of wood on her back up this extremely steep mountain. She was almost bent over at the waist as she climbed. You could see the struggle and the hardship on her face. In that moment I cried out to God for her and others like her who are facing such tremendous hardships.

This woman was persevering because she had no other options. There were no other recourses before her. She had to do what was necessary to keep surviving. I said to the Lord, "I know it was never your plan for humanity to struggle so hard to survive life, please help your children." In that moment, I felt the intense love and compassion of the Father for His children. His love was deep and powerful, and I asked, "What do you want me to pray?" Have you ever spent any time asking God what is on His heart and what He wants you to pray for? I encourage you to ask Him. You will find He has a prayer agenda —things you can pray about daily. Things that are crucial for the lives of His children, not only those in your home but in communities around the world.

Perseverance is not a 'one-time' thing, it is constant. You have to keep at it until you overcome it. People who persevere will succeed because they refuse to give up even when the odds are against them.

Our Christian life is a race. We are not jogging aimlessly but have a purpose for being in the race—eternity with Jesus. We are not in a full-out run to the finish line; we are sprinting to it day by day as we race to gain the prize. Therefore, it will take perseverance and endurance to finish your course well. Do not allow life's difficulties or trials to disqualify you from finishing your race well. Your goal is to cross the finish line into the bosom of the Savior.

> 1 Corinthians 9:24-27 says, "*Do you not know that in a race all the runners run, but only one gets the prize? Run in such a way as to get the prize. Everyone who competes in the games goes into strict training. They do it to get a crown that will not last, but we do it to get a crown that will last forever. Therefore I do not run like a man running aimlessly; I do not fight like a man beating the air. No, I beat my body and make it my slave so that after I have preached to others, I myself will not be disqualified for the prize.*"

Did you notice in the scripture you are the only one who can run your race successfully? And did you also see you are the only one who can disqualify yourself from finishing the race? No matter the obstacles you are facing, the one thing you must be sure of is this—you have already WON. You have won because Jesus won it all for you. He went to the cross and He conquered death, hell, and the grave. Be confident of this: He who began a good work in you will carry it on to completion until the day of Christ Jesus. He will finish what He started in you and will not leave you incomplete. He will not leave you struggling where He finds you but will accomplish His work through you. The suffering, struggles, and hardships you are persevering through will produce good results in your life. Run the race; stay on the course; finish well. Don't disqualify yourself. You will then receive a glorious welcome at the end of your race.

———

A Prayer - Trusting God

Lord, there are seasons when I wonder where You are. Are You with me? Do You hear me? Do You see my distress? Yet, in other seasons, I am reminded You have been with me all along and I can trust You. I remember You have seen me through one difficulty after another. I remember when I thought I would not make it, You showed me I could and would.

When I look back over my life, I am amazed at the many things I have overcome. In my brokenness when I reached for You, You were always there to comfort me. Why then do I struggle with believing You? Why do I lack faith in Your promises? Why do I allow myself to become burdened with fear? Why do I so quickly forget You are with me? Is it because I fail to trust You in all things? Remind me You have been my anchor in every stormy event in my life. You have been my rock and my safe place—my place of refuge from the storms. Help me to trust wholly in You at all times.

Hear my voice when I call, Lord; be merciful to me and answer me. My heart says of you, "Seek his face!" Your face, Lord, I will seek. Do not hide your face from me, do not turn your servant away in anger; you have been my helper. Do not reject me or forsake me, God my Savior. Though my father and mother forsake me, the Lord will receive me. Teach me your way, Lord;

lead me in a straight path. I remain confident of this; I will see the goodness of the Lord in the land of the living. Wait for the Lord; be strong and take heart and wait for the Lord.

Psalm 27:7-14 (NIV)

Father, I am confident as I trust You more and more, I will discover Your goodness is always with me and I will experience this goodness for the rest of my life. Father, as I wait on You, teach me how to take heart in every trying situation because You are with me and You are trustworthy.

Lord, thank You that You do REMEMBER ME. Thank You for redeeming me from every pit I have been in, even those of my own making. You have been faithful, steadfast, and sure. I will remember Your goodness all the days of my life. Thank You for redeeming me from every trouble, unharmed. I CAN TRUST YOU.

Amen – So Be It.

Purchase now: You Can TRUST Him

About the Author

Joan Murray is committed to helping people discover their destinies. She is the founder and CEO of Joan Murray Ministries and Seeds of Hope Worldwide Missions. Joan is dedicated to teaching, training, equipping, and helping people with various life struggles.

Joan is a minister, Bible teacher, author, and missionary. She has traveled extensively throughout the United States and internationally sharing the gospel message and serving the needs of the oppressed. Joan currently resides in Houston, Texas.

If you would like to know more about Joan Murray Ministries or Seeds of Hope Worldwide Missions, please get in touch with us at:

Joan Murray Ministries & Seeds Of Hope Worldwide Missions
26340 FM 1736
Waller, TX 77848
281-398-2501
email: jmmcontactus@gmail.com
website: www.jemmuniquegifts.com
website: www.joanmurrayministries.org

Changing Lives Through the Power and Truth of God's Word.

www.ingramcontent.com/pod-product-compliance
Lightning Source LLC
Chambersburg PA
CBHW071318120626
46546CB00002B/375